Preparation for the Arkansas End-of-Course Exam for Geometry

Copyright © 2006 by McDougal Littell, a division of Houghton Mifflin Company.
All rights reserved.

Permission is hereby granted to teachers to reprint or photocopy in classroom
quantities the pages or sheets in this work that carry a McDougal Littell, a division
of Houghton Mifflin Company, copyright notice. These pages are designed to be
reproduced by teachers for use in their classes with accompanying McDougal
Littell, a division of Houghton Mifflin Company, material, provided each copy made
shows the copyright notice. Such copies may not be sold and further distribution
is expressly prohibited. Except as authorized above, prior written permission must
be obtained from McDougal Littell, a division of Houghton Mifflin Company, to
reproduce or transmit this work or portions thereof in any other form or by any
other electronic or mechanical means, including any information storage or retrieval
system, unless expressly permitted by federal copyright laws. Address inquiries to
Supervisor, Rights and Permissions, McDougal Littell, a division of Houghton Mifflin
Company, P.O. Box 1667, Evanston, IL 60204.

ISBN-13: 978-0-618-62636-6   ISBN-10: 0-618-62636-0

5 6 7 8 9—MJT—10 09 08

Contents

Notes to the Student iv

Correlation Chart C1

Standards Practice Pages 1

Test-Taking Tips 61

Practice Test 63

Diagnostic Score Sheet 85

Notes to the Student

Student Learning Expectations Correlation Presents the Arkansas Mathematics Curriculum Frameworks Student Learning Expectations for Geometry, lists the lessons from *McDougal Littell's Geometry* and *Geometry Concepts & Skills* which cover the given Learning Expectation, and indicates which workbook pages provide practice for the topic.

Learning Expectation Practice Pages Presents a mixture of multiple choice and open response items that directly cover the Learning Expectations for Geometry.

End-of-Course Practice Test Provides a practice test built to closely mirror the design and layout of the Arkansas End-of-Course Test for Geometry.

Diagnostic Scoring Sheet Lists the End-of-Course practice test item that covers each Learning Expectation as well as providing a tally box to track performance and suggested remediation from *Geometry* and *Geometry Concepts & Skills*.

Arkansas Learning Expectations	McDougal Littell Geometry	McDougal Littell Geometry Concepts & Skills	Practice Pages
LG.1.G.1 Define, compare and contrast inductive reasoning and deductive reasoning for making predictions based on real world situations: • venn diagrams • matrix logic • conditional statements (statement, inverse, converse, and contrapositive)	1.1 2.1 2.3	1.2 2.5 3.5	1–2
LG.1.G.2 Represent points, lines, and planes pictorially with proper identification, as well as basic concepts derived from these undefined terms, such as segments, rays, and angles	1.2 1.3 1.4	1.3 1.4 1.5 1.6	3–4
LG.1.G.3 Describe relationships derived from geometric figures or figural patterns	9.4	6.1 6.2 6.3 6.4 6.5 6.6 8.5	5–6
LG.1.G.4 Apply, with and without appropriate technology, definitions, theorems, properties, and postulates related to such topics as complementary, supplementary, vertical angles, linear pairs, and angles formed by perpendicular lines	1.6 2.2 2.6	2.3 2.4 3.2 3.3	7–8
LG.1.G.5 Explore, with and without appropriate technology, the relationship between angles formed by two lines cut by a transversal to justify when lines are parallel	3.3 3.4 3.5	3.5 3.6	9–10
LG.1.G.6 Give justification for conclusions reached by deductive reasoning	2.5 2.6 3.2 3.4 4.3 4.4 4.7 6.3	5.2 5.3	11–12

Preparation for the Arkansas End of Course Exam for Geometry

Arkansas Learning Expectations	McDougal Littell Geometry	McDougal Littell Geometry Concepts & Skills	Practice Pages
T.2.G.1 Apply congruence (SSS . . .) and similarity (AA . . .) correspondences and properties of figures to find missing parts of geometric figures and provide logical justification	4.3 4.4 4.5 8.3 8.4 8.5 8.6	5.1 5.2 5.3 5.4 5.5 7.2 7.3 7.4 7.5	13–14
T.2.G.2 Investigate the measures of segments to determine the existence of triangles (triangle inequality theorem)	5.5 9.3	4.7	15–16
T.2.G.3 Identify and use the special segments of triangles (altitude, median, angle bisector, perpendicular bisector, and midsegment) to solve problems	5.2 5.3 5.4	4.6 5.6 7.5	17–18
T.2.G.4 Apply the Pythagorean Theorem and its converse in solving practical problems	9.2 9.3	4.4 4.5	19–20
T.2.G.5 Use the special right triangle relationships (30°-60°-90° and 45°-45°-90°) to solve problems	9.4	10.2 10.3	21–22
T.2.G.6 Use trigonometric ratios (sine, cosine, tangent) to determine lengths of sides and measures of angles in right triangles including angles of elevation and angles of depression	9.5 9.6	10.4 10.5 10.6	23–24
M.3.G.1 Calculate probabilities arising in geometric contexts (Ex. Find the probability of hitting a particular ring on a dartboard.)	11.6	pp. 713–714	25–26
M.3.G.2 Apply, using appropriate units, appropriate formulas (area, perimeter, surface area, volume) to solve application problems involving polygons, prisms, pyramids, cones, cylinders, spheres as well as composite figures, expressing solutions in both exact and approximate forms	11.2 12.2 12.3 12.4 12.5 12.6	7.2 8.3 8.4 8.5 8.6 9.2 9.3 9.4 9.5 9.6	27–28

Arkansas Learning Expectations	McDougal Littell Geometry	McDougal Littell Geometry Concepts & Skills	Practice Pages
M.3.G.3 Relate changes in the measurement of one attribute of an object to changes in other attributes (Ex. How does changing the radius or height of a cylinder affect its surface area or volume?)	12.2 12.3	9.2 9.3 9.5 9.6	29–30
M.3.G.4 Use (given similar geometric objects) proportional reasoning to solve practical problems (including scale drawings)	8.3 8.4 8.5 8.6 8.7 11.3	7.2 7.3 7.4 7.6	31–32
M.3.G.5 Use properties of parallel lines and proportional reasoning to find the lengths of segments	8.6	7.1 7.2 7.3 7.5	33–34
R.4.G.1 Explore and verify the properties of quadrilaterals	6.1 6.2 6.3 6.4 6.5 6.6	6.1 6.2 6.3 6.4 6.5 6.6	35–36
R.4.G.2 Solve problems using properties of polygons: • sum of the measures of the interior angles of a polygon • interior and exterior angle measure of a regular polygon or irregular polygon • number of sides or angles of a polygon	6.1 6.2 6.5	8.2	37–38
R.4.G.3 Identify and explain why figures tessellate	Project for Chapters 6 and 7 pp. 452–453	Project for Chapters 5 and 6 pp. 352–353	39–40
R.4.G.4 Identify the attributes of the five Platonic Solidss	12.1	9.1 9.3	41–42
R.4.G.5 Investigate and use the properties of angles (central and inscribed) arcs, chords, tangents, and secants to solve problems involving circles	10.1 10.2 10.3 10.4	11.1 11.2 11.3 11.4 11.5 11.6	43–44

Copyright © by McDougal Littell, a division of Houghton Mifflin Company.

Preparation for the Arkansas End of Course Exam for Geometry C3

Arkansas Learning Expectations	McDougal Littell Geometry	McDougal Littell Geometry Concepts & Skills	Practice Pages
R.4.G.6 Solve problems using inscribed and circumscribed figures	5.2 10.3 10.4 11.5 12.3	11.5	45–46
R.4.G.7 Use orthographic drawings (top, front, side) and isometric drawings (corner) to represent three dimensional objects	Project for Chapters 2 and 3 pp. 188–189	3.1 9.1 9.2 9.3 9.4 9.5	47–48
R.4.G.8 Draw, examine, and classify cross-sections of three dimensional objects	12.1 12.4 12.6	9.6	49–50
CGT.5.G.1 Use coordinate geometry to find the distance between two points, the midpoint of a segment, and the slopes of parallel, perpendicular, horizontal, and vertical lines	1.3 1.5 3.6 3.7	2.1 3.6 4.4	51–52
CGT.5.G.2 Write equations of lines in slope-intercept form and use slope to determine parallel and perpendicular lines	3.6 3.7	3.6	53–54
CGT.5.G.3 Determine, given a set of points, the type of figure based on its properties (parallelogram, isosceles triangle, trapezoid)	6.4 6.5 6.6	6.3 6.6	55–56
CGT.5.G.4 Write, in standard form, the equation of a circle given a graph on a coordinate plane or the center and radius of a circle	10.6	11.7	57–58
CGT.5.G.5 Draw and interpret the results of transformations and successive transformations on figures in the coordinate plane: • translations • reflections • rotations (90°, 180°, clockwise and counterclockwise about the origin) • dilations (scale factor)	7.1 7.2 7.3 7.4 7.5 8.7	3.7 5.7 7.6 11.8	59–60

C4 **Preparation for the Arkansas End of Course Exam for Geometry**

Copyright © by McDougal Littell, a division of Houghton Mifflin Company.

Name _____ **Period** _____ **Date** _____

LG.1.G.1

Define, compare and contrast inductive reasoning and deductive reasoning for making predictions based on real world situations
- venn diagrams
- matrix logic
- conditional statements (statement, inverse, converse, and contrapositive)

MULTIPLE CHOICE

1. Given these statements: "The last 12 times that two famous people were married, a third famous person was married within a week. Two famous people were married yesterday." Which of the following statements follows from inductive reasoning?

  Ⓐ Only famous people will be married within a week.

  Ⓑ No famous person will be married within a week.

  Ⓒ Someone will be married within a week.

  Ⓓ Another famous person will be married within a week.

2. Given the conjecture: All mammals cannot fly. What statement is a counterexample to the conjecture?

  Ⓐ Robins are not mammals, and robins can fly.

  Ⓑ Bats are mammals, and bats can fly.

  Ⓒ Dogs are mammals, and dogs cannot fly.

  Ⓓ Lizards are not mammals, and lizards cannot fly.

3. Given the statement, "If the sum of the measures of $\angle A$ and $\angle B$ is 180, then $\angle A$ and $\angle B$ are supplementary," which one of the following is true?

  Ⓐ Only the conditional is true.

  Ⓑ Only the conditional and contrapositive are true.

  Ⓒ Only the converse and inverse are true.

  Ⓓ The conditional, converse, inverse, and contrapositive are all true.

4. What is the converse of "If the team does not win the game on Friday, they will not qualify for the tournament?"

  Ⓐ If we do not qualify for the tournament, we did not win Friday's game.

  Ⓑ If we do not win the game on Friday, we will not qualify for the tournament.

  Ⓒ If we qualify for the tournament, we won the game on Friday.

  Ⓓ If we won the game on Friday, we qualified for the tournament.

5. What is the contrapositive of the conditional statement $m \rightarrow n$?

  Ⓐ $\sim n \rightarrow \sim m$ Ⓑ $\sim m \rightarrow \sim n$

  Ⓒ $n \rightarrow m$ Ⓓ $n \rightarrow \sim m$

Preparation for the Arkansas End of Course Exam for Geometry

Use the table below to answer questions 6, 7, and 8.

Fact	Statement
i.	Jack, Liv, Kate, and Antonio are student council officers.
ii.	The council has 4 officers: president, vice president, secretary, and treasurer.
iii.	Jack is neither president nor secretary.
iv.	A boy holds the office of vice president.
v	Liv is not secretary.
vi.	The names of the treasurer and the vice president have the same number of letters.

6. Who is the president?

  (A) Jack   (B) Liv

  (C) Kate   (D) Antonio

7. Who is the vice president?

  (A) Jack   (B) Liv

  (C) Kate   (D) Antonio

8. Who, respectively, are the secretary and the treasurer?

  (A) Jack and Antonio

  (B) Liv and Kate

  (C) Kate and Liv

  (D) Antonio and Kate

OPEN RESPONSE

A Consider that assertions may be based on either inductive reasoning or deductive reasoning.

  1. How does inductive reasoning differ from deductive reasoning.

  2. What is an example of inductive reasoning?

B Consider the relationships of the following groups: animals, quadrupeds (four-footed animals), dogs, and humans.

  1. Within each group, which of the others are completely contained inside it?

  2. How would a Venn diagram show these relationships?

Name _____ Period _____ Date _____

LG.1.G.2

Represent points, lines, and planes pictorially with proper identification, as well as basic concepts derived from these undefined terms, such as segments, rays, and angles.

MULTIPLE CHOICE

1. Which one of the following statements is false?

   Ⓐ A line contains at least two points.

   Ⓑ Through any two distinct points there exists exactly one line.

   Ⓒ Any three points lie on a distinct line.

   Ⓓ Three non-collinear points determine a plane.

Use the figure to to answer question 2

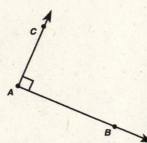

2. Which description best explains what is shown in the figure?

   Ⓐ Two rays that are perpendicular

   Ⓑ Two lines that are perpendicular

   Ⓒ $AB = AC$

   Ⓓ A straight angle

3. Plane P contains points K, L, and M, but not point N. Which of the following represents the intersection of P with the plane that contains points K, L, and N?

   Ⓐ $\overleftrightarrow{KL}$ Ⓑ $\overleftrightarrow{KN}$

   Ⓒ $\overleftrightarrow{LN}$ Ⓓ $\overleftrightarrow{MN}$

4. $\overrightarrow{PR}$ is represented by which sketch?

   Ⓐ    Ⓑ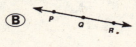

   Ⓒ    Ⓓ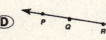

5. What is the notation for the length of the segment between P and Q?

   Ⓐ $\overrightarrow{QP}$ Ⓑ $\overleftrightarrow{PQ}$

   Ⓒ $\overline{PQ}$ Ⓓ PQ

Use the figure below to answer question 6

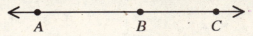

6. If $AB = 18$ and $AC = 31$, what is the length of $\overline{BC}$?

   Ⓐ 49   Ⓑ 31

   Ⓒ 18   Ⓓ 13

Use the figure to answer question 7

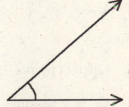

7. What appears to be the correct classification for the angle shown in the figure?

   Ⓐ right   Ⓑ acute

   Ⓒ obtuse   Ⓓ straight

Use the figure to answer question 8

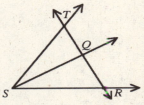

8. Assume $\angle TSR$ is not a straight angle. What three points are collinear?

   Ⓐ points T, Q, and R

   Ⓑ points T, Q, and S

   Ⓒ points S, Q, and R

   Ⓓ points T, S, and R

OPEN RESPONSE

A Draw three noncollinear points, A, B, and C. Then draw point D on line AB between points A and B. Draw segment CD. Draw ray CA and ray CB.

1. Are points A, B, and D collinear? Are points B, C, and D collinear?

2. Are $\overrightarrow{CA}$ and $\overrightarrow{CB}$ opposite rays? Are $\overrightarrow{DA}$ and $\overrightarrow{DB}$ opposite rays?

B Distinct points A, B, and C may be anywhere throughout space.

1. Is it possible for all of points A, B, and C to lie in more than one plane? If so, under what condition can this occur?

2. Is it possible for all of points A, B, and C to lie in more than one plane if $AB \perp AC$? If so, how? If not, why not?

LG.1.G.3
Describe relationships derived from geometric figures or figural patterns.

MULTIPLE CHOICE

1. What is the next number in the sequence?
   −75; −71; −63; −47; . . .
   - Ⓐ −15
   - Ⓑ −29
   - Ⓒ −33
   - Ⓓ −39

2. What is the next number in the sequence?
   −11; −17; −15; −21; . . .
   - Ⓐ −11
   - Ⓑ −15
   - Ⓒ −19
   - Ⓓ −23

Use the figure below to answer question 3.

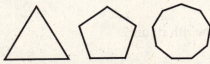

3. In this sequence of figures, how many sides should the next shape in sequence have?
   - Ⓐ 10
   - Ⓑ 11
   - Ⓒ 13
   - Ⓓ 15

Use the figure below to answer question 4.

4. In this sequence of figures, how many sides should the next shape in sequence have?
   - Ⓐ 6
   - Ⓑ 5
   - Ⓒ 4
   - Ⓓ 3

Use the figure to answer question 5.

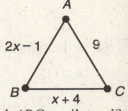

5. For what value of x is $\triangle ABC$ equilateral?
   - Ⓐ 9
   - Ⓑ 5
   - Ⓒ 1
   - Ⓓ none

Use the figure below to answer question 6.

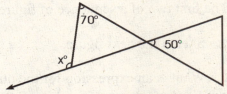

6. In the figure, what is the value of x?
   - Ⓐ 110°
   - Ⓑ 120°
   - Ⓒ 130°
   - Ⓓ cannot determine

Use the figure to answer question 7.

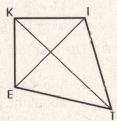

7. Quadrilateral KITE is a kite. What best describes the relationship of segments $\overline{KT}$ and $\overline{EI}$?
   - Ⓐ $KT = EI$
   - Ⓑ $\overline{KT}$ and $\overline{EI}$ are parallel
   - Ⓒ $\overline{KT}$ is a perpendicular bisector of $\overline{EI}$
   - Ⓓ $\overline{EI}$ is a perpendicular bisector of $\overline{KT}$

Preparation for the Arkansas End of Course Exam for Geometry

Use the figure below to answer question 8.

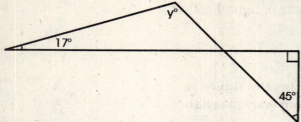

8. In the figure, what is the value of *y*?

   Ⓐ 118° Ⓑ 125°

   Ⓒ 142° Ⓓ 153°

OPEN RESPONSE

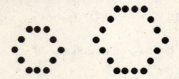

A The first two of a sequence of figures are shown above.

1. Sketch the next figure.

2. What is an expression for the number of dots in the *n*th figure?

$$1$$
$$1 + 3 + 1$$
$$1 + 3 + 5 + 3 + 1$$
$$1 + 3 + \ldots (2n - 3) + (2n - 1) + (2n - 3) + \ldots + 1$$

B The first four expressions describing a sequence of sums are shown above.

1. What are the first three sums in the sequence and what conjecture can you make about the pattern of the given sums?

2. Find the sum of the 6th row.

Preparation for the Arkansas End of Course Exam for Geometry

LG.1.G.4

Apply, with and without appropriate technology, definitions, theorems, properties, and postulates related to such topics as complementary, supplementary, vertical angles, linear pairs, and angles formed by perpendicular lines.

MULTIPLE CHOICE

Use the figure to answer questions 1 and 2.

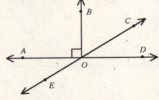

1. Which angle or angles are adjacent to ∠BOC?

   Ⓐ ∠DOE
   Ⓑ ∠DOB
   Ⓒ ∠BOA, ∠BOE and ∠COD
   Ⓓ ∠COD and ∠AOE

2. Which angle or angles are complementary to ∠COD.

   Ⓐ ∠DOE
   Ⓑ ∠BOC
   Ⓒ ∠AOC and ∠DOE
   Ⓓ ∠DOC and ∠AOE

Use the figure to answer question 3.

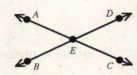

3. If m∠AED = 122°, which of the following statements is false?

   Ⓐ ∠BEC and ∠CED are adjacent angles.
   Ⓑ ∠AEB and ∠DEC are vertical angles.
   Ⓒ m∠BEC = 58°
   Ⓓ m∠AEB = 58°

4. If ∠1 and ∠2 form a linear pair and m∠2 = 67°, what is m∠1?

   Ⓐ 23°   Ⓑ 33°
   Ⓒ 67°   Ⓓ 113°

5. Let ∠1 and ∠2 be supplementary angles and let ∠1 and ∠3 be vertical angles. If m∠2 = 72°, then what is m∠3?

   Ⓐ 108°   Ⓑ 72°
   Ⓒ 28°   Ⓓ 18°

Use the figure to answer question 6.

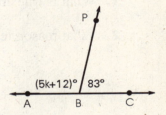

6. ∠PBA and ∠PBC are a linear pair of angles. What is the value of k?

   Ⓐ −6   Ⓑ 12
   Ⓒ 17   Ⓓ 55

Use the figure to to answer question 7.

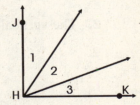

7. Given that m∠1 = m∠3 = 32° and $\overrightarrow{HJ} \perp \overrightarrow{HK}$, what is m∠2?

   Ⓐ 26°   Ⓑ 32°
   Ⓒ 36°   Ⓓ 64°

Preparation for the Arkansas End of Course Exam for Geometry

Use the figure to answer question 8.

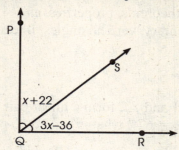

8. If $\overline{PQ} \perp \overline{QR}$, what is the value of *x*?
   - Ⓐ 21
   - Ⓑ 26
   - Ⓒ 31
   - Ⓓ 36

OPEN RESPONSE

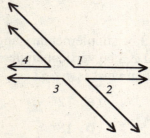

A In the figure, $\angle 1 \cong \angle 3$, $\angle 4$ is supplementary to $\angle 1$, and $\angle 2$ is supplementary to $\angle 3$.

1. What is true about $\angle 2$ and $\angle 4$?

2. What reason leads to the conclusions you reached in question 1?

B Consider the following pairs of vertical angles.

1. The vertical angles also are complementary. What is the measure of one such angle?

2. The vertical angles also are supplementary. What is the measure of one such angle?

8 Preparation for the Arkansas End of Course Exam for Geometry

LG.1.G.5

Explore, with and without appropriate technology, the relationship between angles formed by two lines cut by a transversal to justify when lines are parallel.

MULTIPLE CHOICE

Use the figure below to answer question 1.

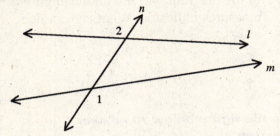

1. What angle relationship best describes ∠1 and ∠2?

   Ⓐ corresponding angles

   Ⓑ consecutive interior angles

   Ⓒ alternate interior angles

   Ⓓ alternate exterior angles

2. What angle relationship best describes ∠6 and ∠2?

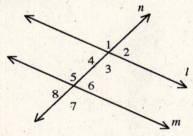

   Ⓐ consecutive interior angles

   Ⓑ corresponding angles

   Ⓒ alternate interior angles

   Ⓓ alternate exterior angles

Use the figure to answer question 3.

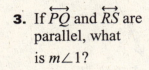

3. If $\overleftrightarrow{PQ}$ and $\overleftrightarrow{RS}$ are parallel, what is $m\angle 1$?

   Ⓐ 108°   Ⓑ 98°

   Ⓒ 72°   Ⓓ 18°

Use the figure below to answer question 4.

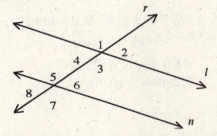

4. In the figure, $l \parallel n$ and r is a transversal. Which of the following is not necessarily true?

   Ⓐ ∠7 ≅ ∠4   Ⓑ ∠2 ≅ ∠6

   Ⓒ ∠8 ≅ ∠2   Ⓓ ∠5 ≅ ∠3

Use the figure to answer question 5.

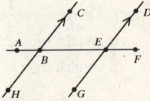

5. In the figure, $m\angle ABC = 125°$. Which statement is false?

   Ⓐ $m\angle GEF = 125°$

   Ⓑ $m\angle DEF = 125°$

   Ⓒ ∠HBF and ∠AED are alternate interior angles

   Ⓓ ∠ABC and ∠AED are corresponding angles

Preparation for the Arkansas End of Course Exam for Geometry   9

Use the figure below to answer question 6.

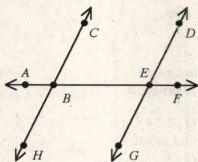

6. In the figure shown, $\overleftrightarrow{HC} \parallel \overleftrightarrow{GD}$ and $m\angle ABC = 113°$. Which of the following statements is false?

Ⓐ $m\angle GEF = 113°$

Ⓑ $m\angle DEF = 67°$

Ⓒ $\angle HBF$ and $\angle AED$ are alternate exterior angles.

Ⓓ $\angle ABH$ and $\angle AEG$ are corresponding angles.

Use the figure below to answer question 7.

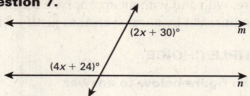

7. In the diagram, $m \parallel n$ with the angle measures indicated. What is the value of x?

Ⓐ 2   Ⓑ 3

Ⓒ 24   Ⓓ 30

Use the figure below to answer question 8.

8. In the diagram, how many lines can be drawn through points A and B parallel to line k?

Ⓐ 0   Ⓑ 1

Ⓒ 2   Ⓓ 3

OPEN RESPONSE

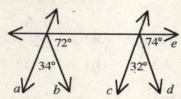

A The diagram above shows an arrangement of lines a, b, c, d, and e.

1. Which pair or pairs of lines are parallel? How do you know this?

2. Which pairs of lines are not parallel?

B A pair of parallel lines intersect a transversal line. An exterior angle formed on one side of the transversal by the first of the parallel lines measures 137°.

1. What is the measure of the angle formed on the other exterior side of the transversal by the second of the parallel lines? Why?

2. What is the measure of the angle formed on the same exterior side of the transversal by the second of the parallel lines? Why?

Name   **Period**   **Date**

LG.1.G.6
Give justification for conclusions reached by deductive reasoning.

MULTIPLE CHOICE

1. Given the following true statements:

  i. No people who make assignments are friendly, and

  ii. All instructors make assignments.

What conclusion logically can be deduced?

  (A) All instructors are friendly.

  (B) Some instructors do not make assignments.

  (C) No instructor is friendly.

  (D) Some instructors are friendly.

2. If $p \rightarrow q$ and $q \rightarrow s$ are true conditional statements, then which one of the following is true?

  (A) $s \rightarrow q$ is valid by the Law of Detachment

  (B) $p \rightarrow s$ is valid by the Law of Syllogism

  (C) $p \rightarrow s$ is valid by the Law of Detachment

  (D) $s \rightarrow p$ is valid by the Law of Syllogism

3. Given the following true statements:

  i. If it is Monday night, Marvin stays at home.

  ii. If Marvin stays at home, he listens to the radio.

Which one of the following statements also must be true?

  (A) If it is not Monday night, Marvin does not listen to the radio.

  (B) If it is not Monday night, Marvin does not stay home.

  (C) If Marvin does not listen to the radio, it is not Monday night.

  (D) If he does not stay home, Marvin does not listen to the radio.

4. In $\triangle LMN$, $\overline{LM} \cong \overline{MN}$. What conclusion may be deduced?

  (A) $\triangle LMN$ is equilateral

  (B) $2LM = LN$

  (C) $\triangle LMN$ is an isosceles triangle

  (D) $LN < LM$

5. Goldbach's conjecture states: every even number greater than 2 can be written as the sum of two primes. Which sum for 30 supports this conjecture?

  (A) $15 + 15$

  (B) $12 + 18$

  (C) $2 + 28$

  (D) $17 + 13$

Use the table below to answer question 6.

$\angle 1$ and $\angle 2$ are a linear pair	Given
$\angle 1$ and $\angle 2$ are supplementary	?

6. What is the theorem or postulate that provides the best justification for the second step of the above argument?

  (A) Congruent Supplements Theorem

  (B) Vertical Angles Theorem

  (C) Congruent Complements Theorem

  (D) Linear Pair Postulate

Preparation for the Arkansas End of Course Exam for Geometry   **11**

7. In △LMN, $\overline{LM} \cong \overline{MN}$. what conclusion may be deduced?

   Ⓐ △LMN cannot be a triangle
   Ⓑ 2LM > LN
   Ⓒ 2LM = LN
   Ⓓ LN < LM

8. A right angle has a measure of 90°. If ∠A is a right angle, what conclusion may be drawn?

   Ⓐ ∠A has measure 180°
   Ⓑ ∠A has measure 90°
   Ⓒ ∠A is complimentary to a 90° angle
   Ⓓ ∠A cannot be supplementary to any angle

OPEN RESPONSE

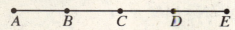

A The illustration above shows five collinear points. It is given that BC = CD and AB = DE. Prove AC = CE.

Statements	Reasons
BC = CD, AB = DE	Given
BC + AB = CD + AB	
BC + AB = CD + DE	
BC + AB = AC, CD + DE = CE	
AC = CE	

1. What reasons justify BC + AB = CD + AB and BC + AB = CD + DE?

2. What reasons justify BC + AB = AC and CD + DE = CE, and AC = CE?

B Given the conjecture, "The altitude from a vertex to the opposite side of a triangle lies within the triangle,"

1. Draw a diagram illustrating the conjecture.

2. Draw a counterexample diagram showing the conjecture is not true.

T.2.G.1

Apply congruence (SSS . . .) and similarity (AA . . .) correspondences and properties of figures to find missing parts of geometric figures and provide logical justification.

MULTIPLE CHOICE

Use the figure below to answer question 1.

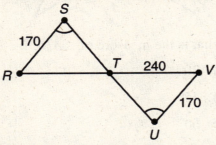

1. Which postulate or theorem can be used to determine the length of $\overline{RT}$?

   Ⓐ SSS Congruence Postulate

   Ⓑ AAS Congruence Theorem

   Ⓒ ASA Congruence Postulate

   Ⓓ SAS Congruence Postulate

2. Given: $\angle B \cong \angle E$ and $\angle C \cong \angle F$. What other piece of information is needed to show $\triangle ABC \cong \triangle DEF$ by ASA Congruence Postulate?

   Ⓐ $\angle A \cong \angle D$

   Ⓑ $\overline{EF} \cong \overline{FE}$

   Ⓒ $\angle B = \angle F$

   Ⓓ $\overline{BC} \cong \overline{EF}$

Use the figure below to answer question 3.

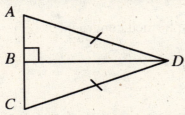

3. What theorem or postulate justifies $\triangle ABD \cong \triangle CBD$?

   Ⓐ SSS

   Ⓑ ASA

   Ⓒ AAS

   Ⓓ HL

Use the figure below to answer question 4.

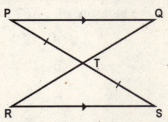

4. Given $\overline{PQ} \parallel \overline{RS}$ and $PT = TS$, which postulate or theorem can be used to prove that $\triangle PQT \cong \triangle RST$?

   Ⓐ SSS

   Ⓑ SAS

   Ⓒ ASA

   Ⓓ AAS

Use the figure below to answer question 5.

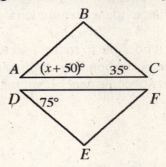

5. In the diagram, $\angle B \cong \angle E$ and $\angle C \cong \angle F$. What is the value of x?

   Ⓐ 25

   Ⓑ 35

   Ⓒ 50

   Ⓓ 75

6. You are given the following information about $\triangle ABC$ and $\triangle DEF$:
   I. $\angle A \cong \angle D$ II. $\angle B \cong \angle E$
   III. $\angle C \cong \angle F$ IV. $\overline{AC} \cong \overline{DF}$

   Which combination cannot be used to prove that $\triangle ABC \cong \triangle DEF$?

   Ⓐ I, II, and III

   Ⓑ I, II, and IV

   Ⓒ I, III, and IV

   Ⓓ II, III, and IV

Preparation for the Arkansas End of Course Exam for Geometry

Use the figure below to answer question 7.

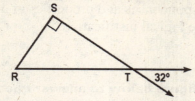

7. What is the measure of ∠SRT?

  Ⓐ 32° Ⓑ 48°
  Ⓒ 58° Ⓓ 108°

Use the figure below to answer question 8.

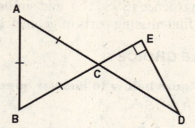

8. What is the measure of ∠ADE?

  Ⓐ 30°
  Ⓑ 45°
  Ⓒ 60°
  Ⓓ cannot be determined

OPEN RESPONSE

A If two corresponding sides and one corresponding angle of two triangles are congruent, the triangles are not necessarily congruent.

  1. What evidence would lead you to conclude that this statement is true?

  2. Is it possible to make a sketch showing how it is possible for two corresponding sides and one corresponding angle of two triangles to be congruent, yet the triangles themselves are not congruent? If so, make such a sketch. Why does your sketch show this?

B A vertical flagpole is supported by wire braces attached to the ground at several points that lie on a circle centered at the base of the flagpole. Each wire brace is attached to the flagpole at the same height. Assume that the ground is a horizontal plane.

  1. Why are the vertical sides and bases of each triangle formed congruent?

  2. Why are the braces all the same length?

T.2.G.2

Investigate the measures of segments to determine the existence of triangles (triangle inequality theorem).

MULTIPLE CHOICE

Use the figure to answer question 1.

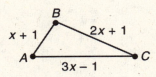

1. Which inequality is a solution for all possible values of x?

   (A) $x > \frac{1}{4}$ (B) $x < \frac{1}{2}$

   (C) $x > \frac{1}{2}$ (D) $x < \frac{1}{4}$

2. Which side lengths allow you to construct a triangle?

   (A) 2, 3, and 8 (B) 6, 8, and 10

   (C) 4, 1, and 9 (D) 7, 2, and 2

3. Two sides of a triangle have lengths 7 and 13. If the length of the third side is given by x, which one of the following is true?

   (A) $6 < x < 20$ (B) $x < 6$

   (C) $6 < x < 13$ (D) $x > 20$

4. Two sides of a triangle have sides 3 and 7. What are the lower and upper bounds for the length of the third side?

   (A) 3 and 11 (B) 2 and 8

   (C) 4 and 10 (D) 3 and 7

5. Which of these lengths could be the sides of a triangle?

   (A) 13 cm, 19 cm, 4 cm

   (B) 19 cm, 9 cm, 11 cm

   (C) 19 cm, 13 cm, 5 cm

   (D) 9 cm, 19 cm, 10 cm

6. A triangle has two sides that have lengths of 12 centimeters and 19 centimeters. Which of the following lengths could not represent the length of the third side?

   (A) 7 centimeters (B) 14 centimeters

   (C) 15 centimeters (D) 19 centimeter

Use the figure below to answer question 7.

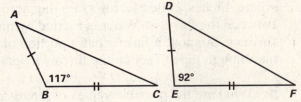

7. Which one of the following statements is always true?

   (A) $AC > DF$ (B) $AC < DF$

   (C) $AC \cong DF$ (D) $m\angle A > m\angle D$

Use the figure below to answer question 8.

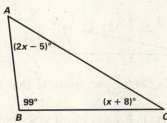

8. Which one of the following correctly lists the sides in order from shortest to longest?

   (A) $BC < AB < AC$

   (B) $AC < BC < AB$

   (C) $AC < AB < BC$

   (D) $AB < BC < AC$

OPEN RESPONSE

A Surface irrigation is one of the most common types of irrigation in which water runs over the surface of a crop field. A specific type of surface irrigation is called furrow irrigation, where ditches, called furrows, are dug across a field and seeds are planted in the ridges between the furrows. Water is carried by pipes and poured out through openings into the furrows. Suppose a farmer has a portion of farmland partially surrounded by trees and only has enough pipe to set up the furrow irrigation as shown in the figure above.

1. What are the possible values of length x? Why?

2. What would happen to $m\angle ABC$ if $\overline{AB}$ is shortened?

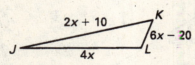

B In the figure above, assume that $m\angle J < m\angle K < m\angle L$.

1. What is the set of all possible values of x?

2. As $m\angle L$ is increased towards 180°, towards what value does x approach?

Name _____ Period _____ Date _____

T.2.G.3
Identify and use the special segments of triangles (altitude, median, angle bisector, perpendicular bisector, and midsegment) to solve problems.

MULTIPLE CHOICE

Use the figure to answer question 1.

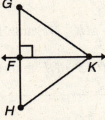

1. If $\overleftrightarrow{KF}$ is the perpendicular bisector of $\overline{GH}$, then which angle is congruent to $\angle KGF$?

   Ⓐ $\angle KHF$ 　　Ⓑ $\angle KFH$
   Ⓒ $\angle FKH$ 　　Ⓓ $\angle FKG$

Use the figure to answer question 2.

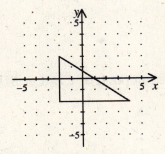

2. For the triangle, find the coordinates of the point of concurrency of the perpendicular bisectors of the sides.

   Ⓐ (2, 0) 　　Ⓑ (1, 0)
   Ⓒ (0, 1) 　　Ⓓ (2, −1)

Use the figure to answer question 3.

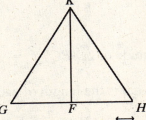

3. In the two-person tent shown below, $\overleftrightarrow{KF}$ is the perpendicular bisector of $\overline{GH}$. What angle must be congruent to $\angle KGF$?

   Ⓐ $\angle KHF$ 　　Ⓑ $\angle KFH$
   Ⓒ $\angle KFG$ 　　Ⓓ $\angle FKG$

4. What is a segment in a triangle called if it connects the midpoints of two sides?

   Ⓐ vertex 　　Ⓑ centroid
   Ⓒ midsegment 　　Ⓓ shortcut

5. How many midsegments does a triangle have?

   Ⓐ 1 　　Ⓑ 2
   Ⓒ 3 　　Ⓓ 4

Use the figure to answer question 6.

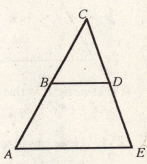

6. Assume B is the midpoint of $\overline{AC}$ and D is the midpoint of $\overline{CE}$. Given $BD = \frac{7}{2}x + 2$ and $AE = 3x + 8$, what is the value of x?

   Ⓐ -1 　　Ⓑ $-\frac{4}{7}$
   Ⓒ 1 　　Ⓓ $\frac{7}{4}$

Use the figure to answer question 7.

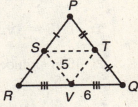

7. For the triangle shown, $VS = 5$ and $VQ = 6$. What is PQ?

   Ⓐ 5 　　Ⓑ 10
   Ⓒ 11 　　Ⓓ 12

Preparation for the Arkansas End of Course Exam for Geometry　17

Use the figure below to answer question 8.

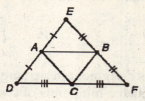

8. For the given triangle, what is the relationships between $\overline{AB}$ and $\overline{DF}$?

   Ⓐ $\overline{AB} \parallel \overline{DF}$ and $AB = 2DF$

   Ⓑ $\overline{AB} \parallel \overline{DF}$ and $AB = DF$

   Ⓒ $\overline{AB} \parallel \overline{DF}$ and $AB = \frac{3}{4}DF$

   Ⓓ $\overline{AB} \parallel \overline{DF}$ and $AB = \frac{1}{2}DF$

OPEN RESPONSE

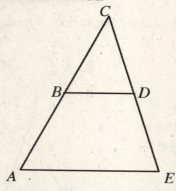

A Assume B is the midpoint of $\overline{AC}$ and D is the midpoint of $\overline{CE}$. Let $BD = 3x + 2$ and $AE = 4x + 8$.

1. How can a solution for x be obtained?

2. What is the value of x?

B Assume that $\triangle ABC$ is an equilateral triangle.

1. If $AB = 8\sqrt{3}$, what is the length of an altitude of $\triangle ABC$?

2. If an altitude of $\triangle ABC$ has length $8\sqrt{3}$, what is the length of each of its sides?

T.2.G.4
Apply the Pythagorean Theorem and its converse in solving practical problems.

MULTIPLE CHOICE

Use the figure to answer question 1.

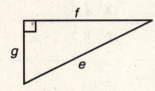

1. For the triangle shown, which of the following equations is true by the Pythagorean Theorem?

   Ⓐ $e^2 + f^2 = g^2$ Ⓑ $e = f + g$
   Ⓒ $f^2 - g^2 = e^2$ Ⓓ $e^2 = f^2 + g^2$

Use the figure to answer question 2.

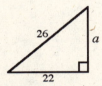

2. What is the approximate value of a to 3 decimal places?

   Ⓐ 4.000 Ⓑ 13.856
   Ⓒ 30.000 Ⓓ 34.059

3. Assuming it is straight, how long is a string reaching from the top of a 20-ft pole to a point 10 ft from the bottom of the pole?

   Ⓐ 30 ft Ⓑ $\sqrt{500}$ ft
   Ⓒ $10 + \sqrt{500}$ ft Ⓓ $30 + \sqrt{500}$ ft

4. How long is a ladder reaching from the top of a 15-ft wall to a point 13 ft from the base of the wall?

   Ⓐ $\sqrt{394}$ ft Ⓑ $\sqrt{404}$ ft
   Ⓒ $\sqrt{66}$ ft Ⓓ $\sqrt{56}$ ft

Use the figure to answer question 5.

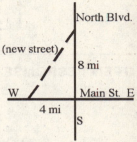

5. The city commission wants to construct a new street that connects Main Street and North Boulevard as shown in the diagram below. The construction cost has been estimated at $120 per linear foot. Find the estimated cost for constructing the street. (1 mile = 5280 ft)

   Ⓐ $1073 Ⓑ $47,226
   Ⓒ $633,600 Ⓓ $5,667,091

6. A radio station is going to construct a 6-foot tower for a new antenna. The tower will be supported by three cables, each attached to the top of the tower and to points on the roof of the building that are 8 feet from the base of the tower. Find the total length of the three cables.

   Ⓐ 50 ft Ⓑ 30 ft
   Ⓒ 10 ft Ⓓ 40 ft

Use the figure to answer question 7.

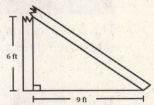

7. A telephone pole breaks and falls as shown. To the nearest foot, what was the original height of the pole?

   Ⓐ 15 ft Ⓑ 17 ft
   Ⓒ 19 ft Ⓓ 21 ft

Use the figure below to answer question 8.

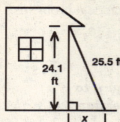

8. A 25.5-foot ladder rests against the side of a house at a point 24.1 feet above the ground. The foot of the ladder is x feet from the house. Find the value of x to one decimal place.

  Ⓐ 1.9   Ⓑ 7.0
  Ⓒ 8.3   Ⓓ 10.1

OPEN RESPONSE

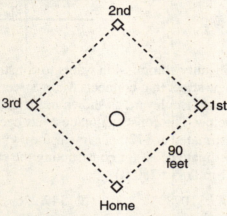

A A baseball "diamond" is a square with a side length of 90 ft.

1. To one decimal place, how far is the throw from third base to first base?

2. To one decimal place, how far is the throw from half-way between home plate and third base to first base?

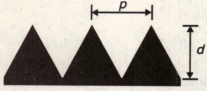

B The cross section of a V-thread on a screw is an equilateral triangle. The distance p between successive threads is known as the pitch of the thread, and the distance d is the depth of the thread.

1. If $p = \frac{1}{8}$ inch, what is d?

2. If $d = \frac{1}{8}$ inch, what is p?

20 Preparation for the Arkansas End of Course Exam for Geometry

Name _____ Period _____ Date _____

T.2.G.5
Use the special right triangle relationships (30°-60°-90° and 45°-45°-90°) to solve problems.

MULTIPLE CHOICE

1. In a 45°-45°-90° triangle, what is the ratio of the length of the hypotenuse to the length of a side?
   - Ⓐ 1:1
   - Ⓑ √2:1
   - Ⓒ √3:1
   - Ⓓ 2:1

Use the figure to answer question 2.

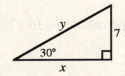

2. What are the values of x and y?
   - Ⓐ 14 and $3\sqrt{7}$
   - Ⓑ 14 and $7\sqrt{3}$
   - Ⓒ $7\sqrt{3}$ and 14
   - Ⓓ $3\sqrt{7}$ and 14

3. The shorter leg of a 30°−60°−90° triangle is 9.4 feet long. What is the perimeter of the triangle?
   - Ⓐ $(18.8 + 9.4\sqrt{3})$ ft
   - Ⓑ $(18.8 + 9.4\sqrt{2})$ ft
   - Ⓒ $(28.2 + 9.4\sqrt{2})$ ft
   - Ⓓ $(28.2 + 9.4\sqrt{3})$ ft

4. Which of the following cannot be the lengths of a 30°-60°-90° triangle?
   - Ⓐ $\frac{5}{2}, 5, \frac{5}{2}\sqrt{3}$
   - Ⓑ $\frac{10}{3}, \frac{20}{3}, \frac{10}{3}\sqrt{3}$
   - Ⓒ 11, 22, $11\sqrt{3}$
   - Ⓓ 3, $\frac{3}{2}$, $3\sqrt{3}$

5. What is the length of an altitude of an equilateral triangle with side lengths $8\sqrt{3}$?
   - Ⓐ 24
   - Ⓑ $8\sqrt{3}$
   - Ⓒ 12
   - Ⓓ $4\sqrt{3}$

6. Which triangle below is NOT congruent to the others?

   Ⓐ
   Ⓑ
   Ⓒ
   Ⓓ

7. What is the length of the diagonal of a square with side lengths $7\sqrt{2}$?
   - Ⓐ $14\sqrt{2}$
   - B 14
   - Ⓒ $7\sqrt{2}$
   - D 7

8. The shortest leg of a 30°-60°-90° triangle is 21 cm long. What are the lengths of the longer side and hypotenuse, rounded to the nearest tenth?
   - Ⓐ side, 29.7 cm; hypotenuse, 31.5 cm
   - Ⓑ side, 31.5 cm; hypotenuse, 29.7 cm
   - Ⓒ side, 42 cm; hypotenuse, 36.4 cm
   - Ⓓ side, 36.4 cm; hypotenuse, 42 cm

Preparation for the Arkansas End of Course Exam for Geometry

OPEN RESPONSE

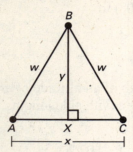

A In the figure, △ABC is isosceles. Answer the following questions and explain your reasoning in each case.

1. What must the ratio of *w* to *y* be to make △ABC equilateral?

2. In △ABC, if $m\angle BAC = 45°$, what must be the ratio of *w* to *x*?

B Imagine that you are creating quilting blocks out of squares.

1. If a block has a side of length 10 centimeters, how long is each diagonal to the nearest tenth of a centimeter?

2. If a block is to have a diagonal of length 10 centimeters, how long must be each side to the nearest tenth of a centimeter?

T.2.G.6

Use trigonometric ratios (sine, cosine, tangent) to determine lengths of sides and measures of angles in right triangles including angles of elevation and angles of depression.

MULTIPLE CHOICE

Use the figure below to answer question 1.

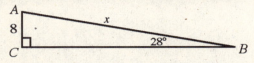

1. Find the value of x, to the nearest whole number. (not drawn to scale)

   Ⓐ 28 Ⓑ 17
   Ⓒ 15 Ⓓ 8

Use the figure to answer question 2.
(not drawn to scale)

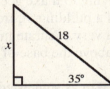

2. What is the value of x to the nearest hundredth?

   Ⓐ 10.32 Ⓑ 12.60
   Ⓒ 14.74 Ⓓ 25.71

3. Assume that ∠A is an acute angle and tan A = 1.230. What is the approximate measure of ∠A to the nearest tenth degree?

   Ⓐ 7.0° Ⓑ 39.1°
   Ⓒ 50.9° Ⓓ 129.9°

4. To the nearest tenth what are the missing angle and side measures of ∠ABC, given that ∠A = 55.0°, ∠C = 90.0°, and CB = 16.0?

   Ⓐ ∠B = 35.0°, AB = 19.5, AC = 11.2
   Ⓑ ∠B = 145.0°, AB = 19.5, AC = 11.7
   Ⓒ ∠B = 145.0°, AB = 19.5, AC = 11.2
   Ⓓ ∠B = 35.0°, AB = 19.0, AC = 11.2

Use the figure below to answer question 5.

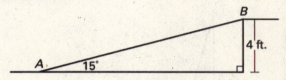

5. The figure shows a ramp leading up to a loading dock that forms a 15° angle with the ground. The loading dock height is 4 feet. What is the approximate distance from point A to point B to the nearest hundredth foot?

   Ⓐ 4.14 feet Ⓑ 14.93 feet
   Ⓒ 15.45 feet Ⓓ 26.67 feet

Use the figure to answer question 6.

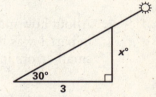

6. When the sun is 30° above the horizon, a stick casts a shadow that is 3 meters long. To the nearest hundredth meter, approximately how tall is the stick?

   Ⓐ 1.50 meters Ⓑ 1.73 meters
   Ⓒ 2.59 meters Ⓓ 3.00 meters

Use the figure to answer question 7.

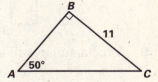

7. The length of $\overline{BC}$ is 11. To the nearest tenth, what is the approximate length of $\overline{AC}$?

   Ⓐ 5.5 Ⓑ 9.2
   Ⓒ 14.4 Ⓓ 15.7

Preparation for the Arkansas End of Course Exam for Geometry

8. A straight slide 3.43 m long makes an angle of 29° with the ground. To the nearest tenth meter, about how much distance does the slide cover along the ground?

   (A) 1.7 m   (B) 1.9 m
   (C) 3.0 m   (D) 3.4 m

OPEN RESPONSE

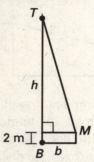

A A transit is an instrument that is used in surveying to make accurate measurements of angles. Suppose you want to find the height of a building, h, from point B to point T as shown in the diagram. You have a transit and a very accurate measuring tape that is only 5 meters long. The transit stands 2.00 meters above the base of the building.

   1. If you measure $\angle M = 84.7°$ when $b = 5.00$ m as suggested by the diagram, what is h?

   2. About how many meters in error is your measurement of h if your measurement of $\angle M$ in part 1 was too high by just 1°? Do you think that this measurement is sensitive to small errors in the measurement of the angle? Why or why not?

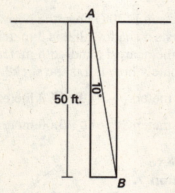

B A rectangular well with parallel sides is dug into the ground to a depth of 50 feet.

   1. An observer at point A looks down to point B at a 10° angle with the nearest wall. What is the approximate width of the well?

   2. The observer checks a second well known to have the same width as the well in the previous question. This time, the angle from the near side at the top to the far side at the bottom is found to be 14°. What is the depth of the second well?

24 Preparation for the Arkansas End of Course Exam for Geometry

M.3.G.1
Calculate probabilities arising in geometric contexts (Ex. Find the probability of hitting a particular ring on a dartboard.).

MULTIPLE CHOICE

1. A friend promises to call you sometime between 4:00 and 4:30 P.M. If you are not home to receive the call until 4:10, what is the probability that you miss the first call that your friend makes to you?

   Ⓐ $\frac{1}{3}$ Ⓑ $\frac{1}{2}$
   Ⓒ $\frac{2}{3}$ Ⓓ 1

2. M is the midpoint of $\overline{AB}$ and Q is the midpoint of $\overline{MB}$. If a point of $\overline{AB}$ is picked at random, what is the probability that the point is on $\overline{QB}$?

   Ⓐ 1 Ⓑ $\frac{3}{4}$
   Ⓒ $\frac{1}{2}$ Ⓓ $\frac{1}{4}$

3. A piece of wire 6 inches long is cut into two pieces at a random point. What is the probability that both pieces of wire will be at least 1 inch long?

   Ⓐ $\frac{11}{12}$ Ⓑ $\frac{5}{6}$
   Ⓒ $\frac{2}{3}$ Ⓓ $\frac{1}{2}$

Use the figure below to answer question 4.

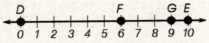

4. What is the probability that a point chosen at random on $\overline{DE}$ is on $\overline{FG}$?

   Ⓐ 100% Ⓑ 70%
   Ⓒ 30% Ⓓ 15%

Use the figure below to answer question 5.

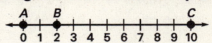

5. What is the probability that a point chosen at random on $\overline{AC}$ is not on $\overline{AB}$?

   Ⓐ $\frac{4}{5}$ Ⓑ $\frac{3}{8}$
   Ⓒ $\frac{1}{4}$ Ⓓ $\frac{1}{5}$

6. A researcher was tape recording birdcalls. The tape recorder had a 1-hour tape in it. Eight minutes after the recorder was turned on, a 5-minute birdcall began. Later, the researcher accidentally erased a continuous 10-minute portion of the tape at a random location. What is the probability that all of the birdcall was erased?

   Ⓐ $\frac{3}{25}$ Ⓑ $\frac{4}{15}$
   Ⓒ $\frac{1}{12}$ Ⓓ $\frac{1}{6}$

Use the diagram below to answer question 7.

7. A and B are the endpoints of a diameter. If C is a point chosen at random from the points on the circle (excluding A and B), what is the probability that $\triangle ABC$ is a right triangle?

   Ⓐ 1 Ⓑ 0.5
   Ⓒ 0.25 Ⓓ 0

Preparation for the Arkansas End of Course Exam for Geometry

Use the diagram below to answer question 8.

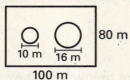

8. Parachutists jump from an airplane and land in the rectangular field shown. Assuming the parachutist is unable to control the landing point, what is the probability that the parachutist avoids the two trees represented by the circles in the diagram?

   A $\dfrac{356\pi}{8000}$ B $\dfrac{89\pi}{8000}$

   C $\dfrac{26\pi}{8000}$ D $\dfrac{\pi}{8000}$

OPEN RESPONSE

A Suppose you have measured the amount of time between snap and down that the ball is actually in play during a football game. This turned out to be 12 seconds for every 1 minute of game-clock time. A game consists of four 15-minute quarters of game-clock time. But, with "time outs" and intermissions, a typical game lasts 3 hours of total elapsed time. Now suppose you turn on your television at a random time during the 3-hour period of a whole game.

1. Based on the given data, what is this probability that you will see a play running between snap and down at the moment you turn on your television?

2. What would a 3-hour clock face showing the probability that actual snap-to-down play is happening at that instant look like?

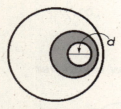

B A target consists of three circles arranged as shown in the diagram above. The innermost circle has diameter d, the middle circle has diameter $2d$, and the outermost circle has diameter $4d$.

1. If a dart is stuck in a random location on the target, what is the probability it is in the innermost circle?

2. If a dart is stuck in a random location on the target, what is the probability it is in the shaded area?

M.3.G.2

Apply, using appropriate units, appropriate formulas (area, perimeter, surface area, volume) to solve application problems involving polygons, prisms, pyramids, cones, cylinders, spheres as well as composite figures, expressing solutions in both exact and approximate forms.

MULTIPLE CHOICE

Use the figure to answer question 1.

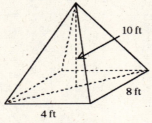

1. The pyramid shown has a rectangular base and faces that are isosceles triangles. What is its volume?

   (A) 152 ft^3 (B) 320 ft^3

   (C) $\frac{512}{3}\sqrt{6} \text{ ft}^3$ (D) $\frac{320}{3} \text{ ft}^3$

Use the figure to answer question 2.

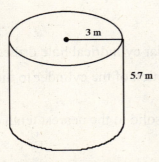

2. What is the surface area of the cylinder to the nearest square unit? Use $\pi \approx 3.14$

   (A) 82 m^2 (B) 26 m^2

   (C) 17 m^2 (D) 164 m^2

3. An aquarium in a restaurant is a rectangular prism and measures 3.5 feet by 4 feet by 4 feet. What is the volume of the aquarium?

   (A) 56 cubic feet   (B) 19.5 cubic feet

   (C) 11.5 cubic feet   (D) 48 cubic feet

Use the figure to answer question 4.

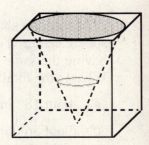

4. A machinist drilled a conical hole into a cube of metal as shown. If the cube has sides of length 6 cm, what is the volume of the metal after the hole is drilled? Use $\pi \approx 3.14$ and round to the nearest tenth.

   (A) 140.6 cm^3 (B) 159.5 cm^3

   (C) 148.2 cm^3 (D) 148.1 cm^3

Use the figure to answer question 5.

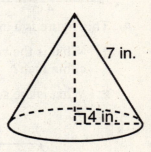

5. What is the surface area of the right cone?

   (A) $44\pi \text{ in.}^2$ (B) $36\pi \text{ in.}^2$

   (C) $16\sqrt{33}\pi \text{ in.}^2$ (D) $112\pi \text{ in.}^2$

6. What is the height of a right cylinder with total surface area of 1036π square feet and radius 14 feet?

   (A) 5.29 feet   (B) 23 feet

   (C) 31.3 feet   (D) 98 feet

Preparation for the Arkansas End of Course Exam for Geometry

Use the figure to answer question 7.

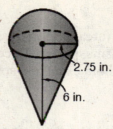

2.75 in.
6 in.

7. This diagram shows the base of a half sphere centered on the base of a cone having the same radius as the half sphere. What is the total volume of the figure?

Ⓐ about 182 in³   Ⓑ about 91.1 in³
Ⓒ about 36.0 in³   Ⓓ about 30.7 in³

8. The surface area of a regular pyramid is 270 cm². Its base is a square with area 81 cm. What is the slant height of the pyramid?

Ⓐ 6.3 cm   Ⓑ 10.5 cm
Ⓒ 20.25 cm   Ⓓ 21 cm

OPEN RESPONSE

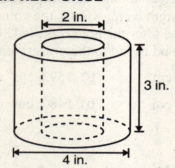

2 in.
3 in.
4 in.

A This figure is a cylindrical solid with a circular cylindrical hole drilled out of the center.

1. What is the volume of the drilled-out portion of the cylinder to the nearest hundredth cubic inch?

2. What is the surface area of the resulting solid to the nearest tenth of a square inch?

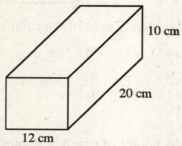

10 cm
20 cm
12 cm

B Ralph bought a generator that will run for 2 hours on a liter of gas. The gas tank on the generator is a rectangular prism with dimensions 12 centimeters by 10 centimeters by 20 centimeters as shown below.

1. What is the volume of the tank?

2. If Ralph fills the tank with gas, how long will the generator run?

Name   **Period**   **Date**

M.3.G.3

Relate changes in the measurement of one attribute of an object to changes in other attributes (Ex. How does changing the radius or height of a cylinder affect its surface area or volume?).

MULTIPLE CHOICE

1. What happens to the volume of a cone if its radius is doubled while its height is halved?

   (A) The volume is not able to be determined.

   (B) The volume is doubled.

   (C) The volume is unchanged.

   (D) The volume is increased by a factor of $\frac{1}{3}$.

2. A glass sphere weighs 0.5lb. How much does another such sphere weigh if its radius is three times as large?

   (A) 13.5 lb   (B) 6.2 lb

   (C) 1.5 lb   (D) 4.5 lb

3. A design on a balloon is 2 cm wide when the balloon holds 65 cm^3 of air. How much must the balloon hold for the design to be 4 cm wide?

   (A) 431 cm^3 (B) 260 cm^3

   (C) 130 cm^3 (D) 520 cm^3

4. The scale factor of two cubes is 2:5. The side length of the smaller cube is 5 cm. What is the volume of the larger cube?

   (A) about 391 cm^3 (B) about 782 cm^3

   (C) about 977 cm^3 (D) about 1950 cm^3

5. Which expression is the ratio of the volume to the surface area of a sphere?

   (A) $\frac{r^2}{2}$ (B) $\frac{r}{2}$

   (C) $\frac{r^2}{3}$ (D) $\frac{r}{3}$

6. Which expression is the ratio of surface area of a sphere of radius r to the surface area of a sphere of radius a?

   (A) $\frac{r^2}{a^2}$ (B) $\frac{r}{a}$

   (C) ra (D) r^2a^2

7. Which expression is the ratio of volume to surface area of a cube with side length s.

   (A) $\frac{s^2}{6}$ (B) $\frac{s}{6}$

   (C) $\frac{s^2}{3}$ (D) $\frac{s}{3}$

8. The volume of a cylinder that is open at both ends increases from 18π to 36π while the height remains constant. By what factor does the surface area of the cylinder increase?

   (A) 1   (B) $\sqrt{2}$

   (C) 2   (D) $2\sqrt{2}$

Preparation for the Arkansas End of Course Exam for Geometry   29

OPEN RESPONSE

A Suppose you are designing a swimming pool. The pool opening plus a deck exactly 5 feet wide must fit in a square area that is 24 feet by 24 feet. The water in the pool is to be 5 feet deep.

1. Sketch two possible shapes for the pool, one with a circular pool opening and one with a square pool opening?

2. Which pool shape would contain more water?

B An official major league baseball has a circumference of 9 inches, while a size 7 basketball has a circumference of 29.5 inches.

1. What is the approximate ratio of the volume of the baseball to the volume of the basketball?

2. What is the approximate ratio of the surface area of the baseball to the surface of the basketball?

Name _____ Period _____ Date _____

M.3.G.4
Use (given similar geometric objects) proportional reasoning to solve practical problems (including scale drawings).

MULTIPLE CHOICE

Use the figure below to answer question 1.

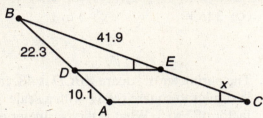

1. What is the value of x to one decimal place?

   Ⓐ 19.0 Ⓑ 22.5
   Ⓒ 0.5   Ⓓ 2.2

Use the figure to answer question 2.

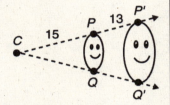

2. What is the scale factor for the dilation shown?

   Ⓐ $\frac{13}{15}$ Ⓑ $\frac{28}{15}$
   Ⓒ $\frac{13}{28}$ Ⓓ $\frac{15}{13}$

Use the figure to answer question 3.

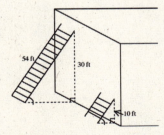

3. Two ladders are leaning against a wall at the same angle as shown. How long is the shorter ladder?

   Ⓐ 36 ft Ⓑ 18 ft
   Ⓒ 8 ft   Ⓓ 22 ft

Use the figure below to answer question 4.

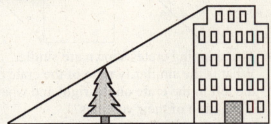

4. Ruby wants to find the height of the tallest building in her city. There is a tree 43 feet in front of her, which she knows is 17 feet tall. She stands 492 feet away from the building and sights the top just at the top of the tree. Which is closest to the height of the building?

   Ⓐ 195 ft Ⓑ 93 ft
   Ⓒ 34 ft   Ⓓ 17 ft

Use the figure below to answer question 5.

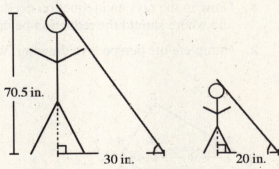

5. At the same time of day, a man who is 70.5 inches tall casts a 30-inch shadow and his son casts a 20-inch shadow. What is the height of the man's son?

   Ⓐ 70.5 in. Ⓑ 50.5 in.
   Ⓒ 47.0 in. Ⓓ 40.5 in.

Preparation for the Arkansas End of Course Exam for Geometry

Use the figure below to answer question 6.

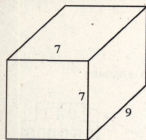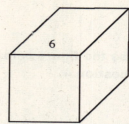

6. The shipping crates shown are similar. What is the similarity ratio of the crate on the left to the crate on the right and what is the ratio of their volumes?

   Ⓐ $\frac{7}{6}$ and $\frac{49}{36}$ Ⓑ $\frac{7}{6}$ and $\frac{343}{216}$

   Ⓒ $\frac{9}{6}$ and $\frac{49}{36}$ Ⓓ $\frac{9}{6}$ and $\frac{343}{216}$

7. You use a pantograph to enlarge a drawing of a tree that is 14 cm high. You want your enlargement to be 56 cm high. What is the scale factor of the enlargement for the drawing?

   Ⓐ 1 to 3   Ⓑ 1 to 4
   Ⓒ 3 to 1   Ⓓ 4 to 1

8. The perimeter of square *ABCD* is 48. It is similar to square *QRST* with a scale factor of 2 to 3. What is the perimeter of square *QRST*?

   Ⓐ 144   Ⓑ 96
   Ⓒ 84   Ⓓ 72

OPEN RESPONSE

A Use the figure to create a perspective drawing with the given polygon, given vanishing point, and dilation of scale factor $\frac{1}{3}$.

  1. Draw in the rays and reduction needed for the perspective drawing. Where should rays and where should the reduction be drawn?

  2. Complete the perspective drawing. What are the steps required to complete the drawing?

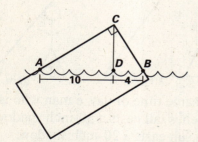

B A rectangular plastic box weighted with sand in one corner is floating in some water. The distance between wave peaks is 2 feet.

  1. Which triangles are similar in this situation?

  2. What is the approximate height of point *C* above the waterline to the nearest tenth foot?

32 Preparation for the Arkansas End of Course Exam for Geometry

M.3.G.5
Use properties of parallel lines and proportional reasoning to find the lengths of segments.

MULTIPLE CHOICE

Use the figure below to answer question 1.

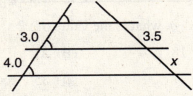

1. What is the value of *x* to one decimal place?
   - Ⓐ 3.8
   - Ⓑ 4.0
   - Ⓒ 4.5
   - Ⓓ 4.7

Use the figure below to answer question 2.

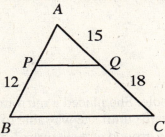

2. Given $\overline{PQ} \parallel \overline{BC}$, what is the length of $\overline{AB}$?
   - Ⓐ 22
   - Ⓑ 18
   - Ⓒ 14
   - Ⓓ 10

Use the figure below to answer question 3.

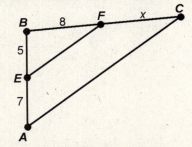

3. If $EF \parallel AC$, what is the value of *x* to one decimal place?
   - Ⓐ 11.2
   - Ⓑ 11.0
   - Ⓒ 9.0
   - Ⓓ 5.7

Use the figure below to answer question 4.

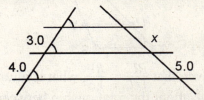

4. What is the value of *x* to one decimal place?
   - Ⓐ 3.8
   - Ⓑ 4.0
   - Ⓒ 4.5
   - Ⓓ 4.7

Use the figure below to answer question 5.

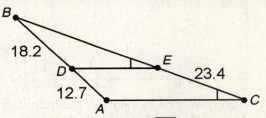

5. What is the length of $\overline{BC}$ to one decimal place?
   - Ⓐ 30.9
   - Ⓑ 33.5
   - Ⓒ 54.1
   - Ⓓ 56.9

Use the figure below to answer question 6.

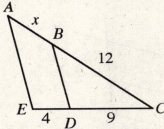

6. In the figure, $\overline{AE} \parallel \overline{BD}$. What is the value of *x*?
   - Ⓐ $\frac{16}{3}$
   - Ⓑ 6
   - Ⓒ $\frac{19}{3}$
   - Ⓓ 7

Preparation for the Arkansas End of Course Exam for Geometry

Use the figure below to answer question 7.

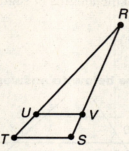

7. Given that $\dfrac{RU}{UT} = \dfrac{RV}{VS}$, what is always true about the relationship between $\overline{UV}$ and $\overline{TS}$?

   Ⓐ $\overline{UV} \perp \overline{TS}$ Ⓑ $\overline{UV} \parallel \overline{TS}$

   Ⓒ $UV = TS$ Ⓓ $UV \neq TS$

Use the figure below to answer question 8.

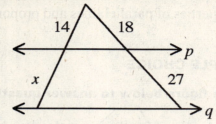

8. If $p \parallel q$, what is the value of x?

   Ⓐ 18   Ⓑ 21

   Ⓒ 27   Ⓓ 35

OPEN RESPONSE

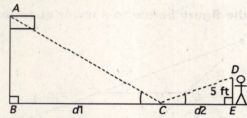

A Karen wanted to measure the height of her school's flagpole. She placed a mirror on the ground d_1 feet from the flagpole, then she walked backwards until she was able to see the top of the pole in the mirror. Her eyes were 5 ft above the ground and she was d_2 ft from the mirror.

1. If $d_1 = 50$ ft and $d_2 = 12$ ft, what is the height of the flagpole the nearest foot?

2. What postulates or theorems prove that $\triangle ABC$ and $\triangle DEC$ are similar? How is the answer computed?

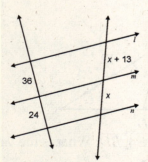

B The figure shows lines l, m, and n cut by two transversals, forming segments with the measures shown.

1. Under what condition is $l \parallel m \parallel n$ true?

2. What must be the value of x in order for $l \parallel m \parallel n$ to be true?

R.4.G.1
Explore and verify the properties of quadrilaterals.

MULTIPLE CHOICE

1. Which statement is true?
   - Ⓐ All quadrilaterals are squares.
   - Ⓑ All rectangles are squares.
   - Ⓒ All rectangles are quadrilaterals.
   - Ⓓ All quadrilaterals are rectangles.

2. Which statement is not always true?
   - Ⓐ For an isosceles trapezoid the diagonals are perpendicular.
   - Ⓑ For an isosceles trapezoid the legs are congruent.
   - Ⓒ For an isosceles trapezoid the diagonals are congruent.
   - Ⓓ For an isosceles trapezoid the base angles are congruent.

Use the figure below to answer question 3.

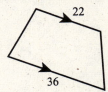

3. For the trapezoid shown below, what is the measure of the midsegment?
   - Ⓐ 25
   - Ⓑ 29
   - Ⓒ 30
   - Ⓓ 58

4. Which type of quadrilateral has no parallel sides?
   - Ⓐ rhombus
   - Ⓑ trapezoid
   - Ⓒ kite
   - Ⓓ rectangle

5. Isosceles trapezoid $JKLM$ has legs $\overline{JK}$ and $\overline{LM}$, and base $\overline{KL}$. If $JK = 4x - 6$, $KL = 2x - 3$, and $LM = 3x - 4$. What is the value of x?
   - Ⓐ $\frac{3}{2}$
   - Ⓑ -10
   - Ⓒ 2
   - Ⓓ 1

Use the figure to answer question 6.

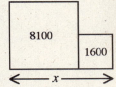

6. This figure is made up of two squares with the areas shown. What is the length of x?
   - Ⓐ 4850
   - Ⓑ 1212.5
   - Ⓒ 130
   - Ⓓ 360

7. Which statement is not always true?
   - Ⓐ For any parallelogram opposite sides are congruent.
   - Ⓑ For any parallelogram the diagonals are perpendicular.
   - Ⓒ For any parallelogram the diagonals bisect each other.
   - Ⓓ For any parallelogram opposite angles are congruent.

8. Which of the following statements is true?
   - Ⓐ Consecutive angles in a parallelogram are always vertical angles.
   - Ⓑ Consecutive angles in a parallelogram are always complementary angles.
   - Ⓒ Consecutive angles in a parallelogram are always supplementary angles.
   - Ⓓ Consecutive angles in a parallelogram are always congruent angles.

OPEN RESPONSE

A Consider the relationships of following geometric figures: quadrilaterals, parallelograms, rectangles, squares, and rhombuses.

1. Within each group, which of the others are completely contained inside it?

2. How would a Venn diagram show the relationships of these figures?

B Consider the statement, "If a parallelogram is a square, then it is a rhombus."

1. Is the statement true or false?

2. Write the converse. Is the converse true or false?

36 Preparation for the Arkansas End of Course Exam for Geometry

R.4.G.2

Solve problems using properties of polygons:
- sum of the measures of the interior angles of a polygon
- interior and exterior angle measure of a regular polygon or irregular polygon
- number of sides or angles of a polygon

MULTIPLE CHOICE

1. Which figure below is not a polygon?

    A   B

    C   D

2. Which one of the statements below is false?

   A) A hexagon has 6 angles.
   B) A pentagon has 8 sides.
   C) A decagon has 10 angles.
   D) A quadrilateral has 4 sides.

Use the figure below to answer question 3.

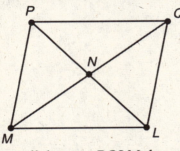

3. For parallelogram PQLM shown, if $m\angle PML = 83°$, then what is $m\angle PQL$?

   A) 97°
   B) 83°
   C) $m\angle QLM$
   D) $m\angle PQM$

Use the figure below to answer question 4.

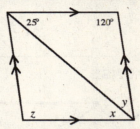

4. What is the value of the variables in the parallelogram?

   A) $x = 35°, y = 25°, z = 120°$
   B) $x = 60°, y = 12.5°, z = 155°$
   C) $x = 25°, y = 35°, z = 120°$
   D) $x = 12.5°, y = 60°, z = 155°$

Use the figure below to answer question 5.

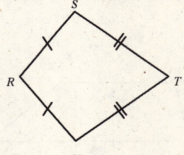

5. If $m\angle R = 110°$ and $m\angle S = 70°$ then what is $m\angle T$?

   A) 110°
   B) 70°
   C) 40°
   D) 20°

6. In the parallelogram QRST, $\angle T = 82°$. What is $m\angle S$?

   A) 41°
   B) 82°
   C) 98°
   D) 139°

Preparation for the Arkansas End of Course Exam for Geometry

7. A convex pentagon has exterior angles that measure 75°, 62°, 68°, and 81°. What is the measure of the exterior angle of the 5th vertex?

   Ⓐ 64°   Ⓑ 74°
   Ⓒ 78°   Ⓓ 84°

Use the figure below to answer question 8.

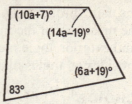

8. What is the value of *a*?

   Ⓐ −3   Ⓑ 9
   Ⓒ 12   Ⓓ 28

OPEN RESPONSE

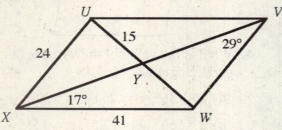

A Given: *UVWX* is a parallelogram, $m\angle WXV = 17°$, $m\angle WVX = 29°$, $XW = 41$, $UX = 24$, $UY = 15$.

1. What is $m\angle WVU$? What is $m\angle XUV$?

2. What is *WV*? What is *UW*?

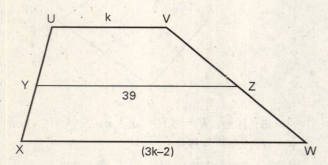

B *UVWX* is a trapezoid with median $\overline{YZ}$.

1. What is the length of $\overline{UV}$?

2. What is the length of $\overline{XW}$?

Name _____ Period _____ Date _____

R.4.G.3
Identify and explain why figures tessellate.

MULTIPLE CHOICE

1. Which of the following polygons can form a regular tessellation?

   Ⓐ regular hexagon
   Ⓑ regular pentagon
   Ⓒ regular octagon
   Ⓓ regular decagon

2. Which of the following figures cannot form a tessellation?

   Ⓐ quadrilateral   Ⓑ hexagon
   Ⓒ ellipse   Ⓓ rectangle

Use the figure below to answer question 3.

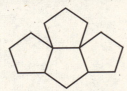

3. Is the figure shown above a tessellation?

   Ⓐ yes
   Ⓑ no
   Ⓒ sometimes
   Ⓓ cannot be determined

4. Which of the following statements is not true?

   Ⓐ A tessellation can be made from a rhombus.
   Ⓑ A tessellation can be made from a trapezoid reflected over its base and then translated.
   Ⓒ A tessellation can be made by translating, rotating, and reflecting a single figure.
   Ⓓ A regular tessellation can be made from a pentagon that is rotated before it is reflected.

5. Regular polygons in a tessellation must fill the plane at each vertex. What does this mean for the interior angles?

   Ⓐ The interior angles of the polygons must add up to 360 degrees.
   Ⓑ The interior angles of the polygons must add up to 180 degrees.
   Ⓒ The interior angles of the polygons cannot exceed 180 degrees.
   Ⓓ Each interior angle of the polygon cannot exceed 60 degrees.

6. Which of the following is not a rule for regular tessellations?

   Ⓐ Regular tessellations must be made of regular polygons that are all the same.
   Ⓑ The polygons in regular tessellations must not overlap.
   Ⓒ Regular tessellations must cover a shape that is not a plane.
   Ⓓ Each vertex of the regular tessellations must look the same.

Preparation for the Arkansas End of Course Exam for Geometry

Use the figure below to answer question 7.

7. Which of the following best describes how the polygon was transformed in the tessellation?

   Ⓐ reflection

   Ⓑ translation

   Ⓒ rotation and translation

   Ⓓ reflection and translation

Use the figure below to answer question 8.

8. Which of the following best describes how the polygon was transformed in the tessellation?

   Ⓐ reflection

   Ⓑ translation

   Ⓒ rotation and translation

   Ⓓ reflection and translation

OPEN RESPONSE

A Sometimes two different polygons can be used to make a tessellation.

1. Can a regular octagon and a square, with all sides from both figures equal in length, be used to make a tessellation? Use words or pictures to explain your answer.

2. Can a regular triangle and a rhombus, with all sides from both figures equal in length, be used to make a tessellation? Use words or pictures to explain your answer.

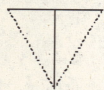

B Because equilateral triangles are one of the few regular polygons that tessellate, you want to cut out different-colored equilateral triangles from construction paper to create a tessellation for the bulletin board. Because you do not want to rely on measuring sixty-degree angles, you decide to create a 'T', in which the leg of the 'T' is the altitude and the top of the 'T' is a side of the triangle. You will then connect the endpoints, as shown above.

1. If you draw a side of length 9 centimeters, how long should the altitude be to the nearest tenth?

2. What is the minimum number of such triangles needed to completely cover an area of dimensions 50 cm × 65 cm?

Name _____ Period _____ Date _____

R.4.G.4
Identify the attributes of the five Platonic Solids.

MULTIPLE CHOICE

Use the diagram to answer question 1.

1. For the above regular tetrahedron, what are the number of faces, vertices, and edges?

    Ⓐ 3 faces, 3 vertices, 5 edges

    Ⓑ 4 faces, 4 vertices, 6 edges

    Ⓒ 4 faces, 6 vertices, 6 edges

    Ⓓ 5 faces, 6 vertices, 8 edges

Use the diagram to answer question 2.

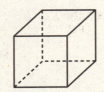

2. For the above regular cube, what are the number of faces, vertices, and edges?

    Ⓐ 6 faces, 8 vertices, 12 edges

    Ⓑ 6 faces, 10 vertices, 10 edges

    Ⓒ 8 faces, 8 vertices, 8 edges

    Ⓓ 8 faces, 10 vertices, 12 edges

Use the diagram to answer question 3.

3. For the above regular octahedron, what are the number of faces, vertices, and edges?

    Ⓐ 4 faces, 6 vertices, 8 edges

    Ⓑ 6 faces, 8 vertices, 10 edges

    Ⓒ 8 faces, 5 vertices, 10 edges

    Ⓓ 8 faces, 6 vertices, 12 edges

Use the diagram to answer question 4.

4. For the above regular dodecahedron, what are the number of faces, vertices, and edges?

    Ⓐ 8 faces, 16 vertices, 24 edges

    Ⓑ 10 faces, 18 vertices, 20 edges

    Ⓒ 12 faces, 20 vertices, 30 edges

    Ⓓ 14 faces, 22 vertices, 28 edges

Use the diagram to answer question 5.

5. For the above regular icosahedron, what are the number of faces, vertices, and edges?

    Ⓐ 16 faces, 8 vertices, 24 edges

    Ⓑ 18 faces, 20 vertices, 22 edges

    Ⓒ 20 faces, 12 vertices, 30 edges

    Ⓓ 22 faces, 11 vertices, 33 edges

6. Which of the following polygons cannot be used in a two-dimensional net that forms a platonic solid?

    Ⓐ regular hexagon

    Ⓑ regular pentagon

    Ⓒ square

    Ⓓ equilateral triangle

Preparation for the Arkansas End of Course Exam for Geometry

7. How many Platonic solids do not have triangular faces?

(A) 1 (B) 2
(C) 3 (D) 4

8. Which is not an attribute of all Platonic solids?

(A) All the faces are paired with an opposing parallel face.

(B) All the vertices are surrounded by the same number of faces.

(C) All faces meet along the edges at the same angle.

(D) All the vertex figures form the same regular polygon.

OPEN RESPONSE

A Euler's theorum states that, for any convex polyhedron, the number of faces (F), vertices (V), and edges (E) are related by the formula $F + V = E + 2$.

1. What equation verifies Euler's formula for the cube?

2. What equation verifies Euler's formula for the tetrahedron?

B The area A of an equilateral triangle is given by the formula $A = \dfrac{\sqrt{3}}{4}s^2$, where s is the length of the side.

1. Using this formula, what is the surface area of a regular tetrahedron of side length s?

2. Using this formula, what is the surface area of a regular icosahedron of side length s?

Name _____ Period _____ Date _____

R.4.G.5
Investigate and use the properties of angles (central and inscribed) arcs, chords, tangents, and secants to solve problems involving circles.

MULTIPLE CHOICE

Use the figure below to answer question 1.

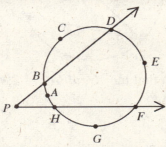

1. In the figure shown (not drawn to scale), $m\widehat{BCD} = 112°$, $m\widehat{DEF} = 98°$, $m\widehat{FGH} = 130°$, and $m\widehat{HAB} = 20°$. What is $m\angle FPD$?

   (A) 20°   (B) 39°
   (C) 16°   (D) 92°

Use the figure below to answer question 2.

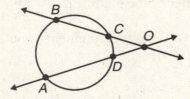

Not drawn to scale

2. Given that $m\widehat{AB} = 82°$, $m\widehat{CD} = 30°$, what is $m\angle DOC$?

   (A) 52°   (B) 56°
   (C) 112° (D) 26°

3. A park maintenance person stands 16 m from a circular monument. If you assume her lines of sight form tangents to the monument and make an angle of 22°, what is the measure of the arc of the monument that her lines of sight intersect?

   (A) 158°   (B) 136°
   (C) 68°   (D) 112°

Use the figure below to answer question 4.

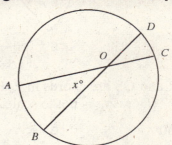

4. What is the value of x if $m\widehat{AB} = 29°$ and $m\widehat{CD} = 35°$?

   (A) 64°   (B) 58°
   (C) 32°   (D) 12°

Use the figure below to answer question 5.

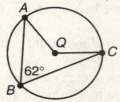

5. Given that $\odot Q$ and $m\angle B = 62°$, what is $m\widehat{AC}$?

   (A) 124°   (B) 236°
   (C) 62°   (D) 248°

Use the figure below to answer question 6.

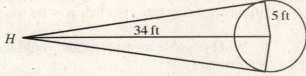

6. A hummingbird is flying toward a large tree with a radius of 5 feet. When it is 34 feet from the center of the tree, its lines of sight form two tangents. What is the measure of the arc on the tree that the hummingbird can see?

   (A) 82.545°   (B) 164.09°
   (C) 81.545°   (D) 163.09°

Preparation for the Arkansas End of Course Exam for Geometry   43

Use the figure to answer question 7.

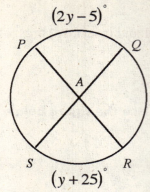

7. If $\overline{PR}$ and $\overline{QS}$ are chords in $\odot A$, what is $m\widehat{PQ}$? (Drawing is not to scale.)

   Ⓐ 60°   Ⓑ 55°
   Ⓒ 50°   Ⓓ 45°

Use the figure below to answer question 8.

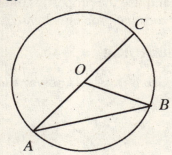

8. Given that in $\odot O$, $m\widehat{BAC} = 296°$, what is $m\angle AOB$?

   Ⓐ 55°   Ⓑ 58°
   Ⓒ 110° Ⓓ 116°

OPEN RESPONSE

A Suppose you needed to measure the diameter of a circular merry-go-round platform. But there were problems because you had no way to reach its center and you had to make the measurement while on the platform. Your only tool was an accurate 3-m measuring tape, but the tape was far too short to reach all the way around the platform.

1. What method could you have used to get the diameter of the platform?

2. Make a sketch showing the necessary measurements. What measurements would have led you to a value of 10 m for the diameter?

B Suppose you made a fairly good estimate of the diameter of a large cylindrical tank from the outside. There was no way you could have reached its center. You had an accurate 10-m measuring tape, but that was far too short to reach all the way around the tank.

1. What possible measurements would have led you to an estimate of 43.2 m for this diameter?

2. Make a sketch showing measurements you could have made to get the diameter of the tank.

R.4.G.6

Solve problems using inscribed and circumscribed figures.

MULTIPLE CHOICE

Use the figure to answer question 1.

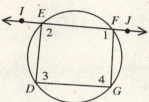

1. Given that $m\angle IED = 94°$ and $m\angle JFG = 92°$, what is the measure of each unknown angle (not drawn to scale)?

   Ⓐ $m\angle 1 = 86°, m\angle 2 = 88°,$
   $m\angle 3 = 92°, m\angle 4 = 94°$

   Ⓑ $m\angle 1 = 88°, m\angle 2 = 86°,$
   $m\angle 3 = 94°, m\angle 4 = 92°$

   Ⓒ $m\angle 1 = 88°, m\angle 2 = 86°,$
   $m\angle 3 = 92°, m\angle 4 = 94°$

   Ⓓ $m\angle 1 = 86°, m\angle 2 = 88°,$
   $m\angle 3 = 94°, m\angle 4 = 92°$

2. A circle can be circumscribed about which quadrilateral?

   Ⓐ   Ⓑ

   Ⓒ 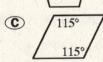   Ⓓ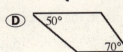

Use the figure to answer question 3.

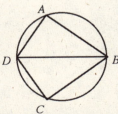

3. Given that $\angle DAB$ and $\angle DCB$ are right angles and $m\overparen{ACB} = 250°$, what is the measure of $\angle ABD$?

   Ⓐ 125°   Ⓑ 55°
   Ⓒ 45°   Ⓓ 35°

Use the figure to answer question 4.

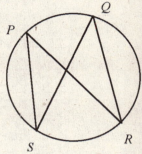

4. Find $m\angle PSQ$ if $m\angle PSQ = 2y - 10$ and $m\angle PRQ = y + 25$.

   Ⓐ 35°   Ⓑ 30°
   Ⓒ 60°   Ⓓ 40°

Use the figure to answer question 5.

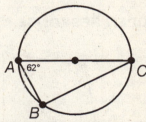

5. Given: $\overline{AC}$ is a diameter of the circle and $m\angle A = 62°$, what is $m\angle ACB$.

   Ⓐ 19°   Ⓑ 28°
   Ⓒ 38°   Ⓓ 62°

Use the figure to answer question 6.

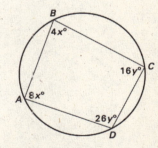

6. What is the measure of $\angle ADC$?

   Ⓐ 52°   Ⓑ 104°
   Ⓒ 130°   Ⓓ 156°

Use the figure below to answer question 7.

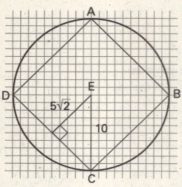

7. What is the area of the inscribed square?

   Ⓐ $200\sqrt{2}$ square units

   Ⓑ $50\pi\sqrt{2}$ square units

   Ⓒ 200 square units

   Ⓓ $100\sqrt{2}$ square units

Use the figure below to answer question 8.

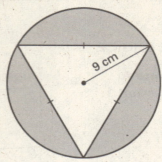

8. An equilateral triangle is inscribed in a circle of radius 9 cm. What is the approximate area of the shaded regions?

   Ⓐ 105.22 cm²   Ⓑ 132.97 cm²

   Ⓒ 149.25 cm²   Ⓓ 173.47 cm²

OPEN RESPONSE

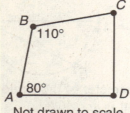

Not drawn to scale

A Quadrilateral ABCD has ∠A and ∠B measures as shown.

1. What must be the measure of ∠C so that a circle may be circumscribed about ABCD?
2. What must be the measure of ∠D so that a circle may be circumscribed about ABCD?

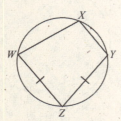

B Quadrilateral WXYZ is inscribed in a circle as shown. It is given that $m\angle X = 100°$, $m\angle Y = 100°$, and $WZ = YZ$.

1. What are the measures of ∠Z and ∠W?
2. What are the measures of $\overarc{WZ}$ and $\overarc{WX}$?

R.4.G.7

Use orthographic drawings (top, front, side) and isometric drawings (corner) to represent three-dimensional objects.

MULTIPLE CHOICE

1. Which view shows the front view of the solid?

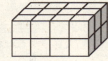

Ⓐ  Ⓑ

Ⓒ 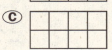 Ⓓ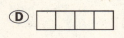

2. Which view shows the side view of the solid?

Ⓐ   Ⓑ

Ⓒ 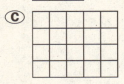 Ⓓ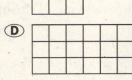

3. Which view shows the side view of the solid?

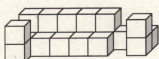

Ⓐ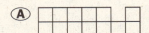

Ⓑ

Ⓒ

Ⓓ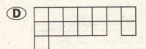

4. Which view shows the top view of the solid?

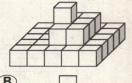

Ⓐ 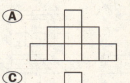 Ⓑ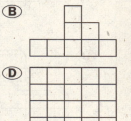

Ⓒ Ⓓ

5. Which solid has the following three views?

Front view   Top view   Side view

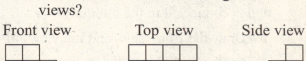

Ⓐ 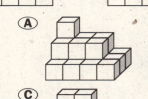 Ⓑ

Ⓒ 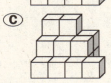 Ⓓ

6. Which solid has the following three views?

Front view   Top view   Side view

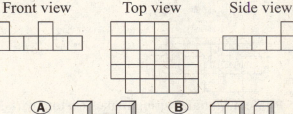

Ⓐ 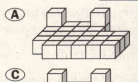 Ⓑ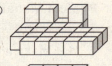

Ⓒ  Ⓓ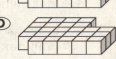

Preparation for the Arkansas End of Course Exam for Geometry

7. Which solid has the following three views?

Front view   Top view   Side view

8. Which solid has the following three views?

Front view   Top view   Side view

OPEN RESPONSE

A A model of a building design is constructed from cubes. The building has two towers and is connected in the middle.

1. Draw the front, side, and top views of the building.
2. On the grid of dots below, make an isometric drawing of the building.

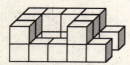

B Zeta Manufacturing makes custom parts, based upon drawings provided by their customers. A customer wants the following part made.

1. Make a drawing of the front view, side view, and top view.
2. If the part was altered as shown, show any changes to the front, top, or side views.

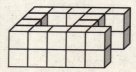

48 Preparation for the Arkansas End of Course Exam for Geometry

R.4.G.8
Draw, examine, and classify cross-sections of three-dimensional objects.

MULTIPLE CHOICE

Use the figure to answer question 1.

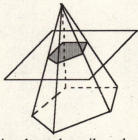

1. Which of the following best describes the cross section?
   - (A) pentagon
   - (B) hexagon
   - (C) pyramid
   - (D) rectangle

Use the figure to answer question 2.

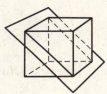

2. Which of the following best describes the cross section?
   - (A) triangle
   - (B) pentagon
   - (C) pyramid
   - (D) rectangle

Use the figure to answer question 3.

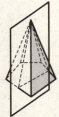

3. Which of the following best describes the cross section?
   - (A) triangle
   - (B) pentagon
   - (C) pyramid
   - (D) rectangle

4. Which of the following best describes a possible cross section of an angel food cake?
   - (A) rectangle
   - (B) trapezoid
   - (C) circle
   - (D) hexagon

5. Which of the following best describes a possible cross section of a telephone book?
   - (A) rectangle
   - (B) trapezoid
   - (C) circle
   - (D) hexagon

Use the figure to answer question 6.

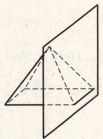

6. Which of the following best describes the cross section?
   - (A) square
   - (B) point
   - (C) isosceles triangle
   - (D) line segment

7. Which of the following statements is false?
   - (A) A plane can intersect a cone in a point.
   - (B) A plane can intersect a cone in an ellipse.
   - (C) A plane can intersect a sphere in a circle.
   - (D) A plane can intersect a sphere in a line segment.

Preparation for the Arkansas End of Course Exam for Geometry

8. Which of the following figures is not a possible cross section of a regular square pyramid?

Ⓐ isosceles trapezoid
Ⓑ equilateral triangle
Ⓒ pentagon
Ⓓ nonsquare rectangle

OPEN RESPONSE

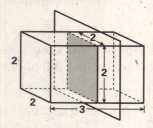

A This figure shows how a plane can intersect a 2″ × 2″ × 3″ rectangular prism to form a 2″ × 2″ square.

1. How can a plane intersect the prism to produce a 2″ × 3″ rectangle?

2. How can a plane intersect the prism to produce a 3″ line segment?

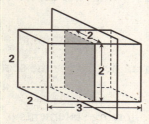

B This figure shows how a plane can intersect a 2″ × 2″ × 3″ rectangular prism to form a 2″ × 2″ square.

1. How can a plane intersect the prism to produce a point?

2. How can a plane intersect the prism to produce a 3″ × 2√2″ rectangle?

CGT.5.G.1
Use coordinate geometry to find the distance between two points, the midpoint of a segment, and the slopes of parallel, perpendicular, horizontal, and vertical lines.

MULTIPLE CHOICE

1. T is the midpoint of $\overline{PQ}$. Which one of the following is not an appropriate statement?
   - Ⓐ $PT + TQ = PQ$
   - Ⓑ $\overline{PT} \cong \overline{TQ}$
   - Ⓒ $\overline{PT} = \overline{TQ}$
   - Ⓓ $PT = TQ$

Use the figure to answer question 2.

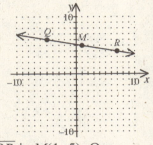

2. The midpoint of $\overline{QR}$ is $M(1, 5)$. One endpoint is $R(7, 4)$. What are the coordinates of the other endpoint?
   - Ⓐ $(-5, 6)$
   - Ⓑ $(5, 6)$
   - Ⓒ $(5, -6)$
   - Ⓓ $(-5, -6)$

3. Which of the following is the slope of a line parallel to one passing through the points $A(-8, -3)$ and $B(-5, -2)$.
   - Ⓐ $\dfrac{1}{3}$
   - Ⓑ 3
   - Ⓒ $\dfrac{5}{13}$
   - Ⓓ 15

Use the figure to answer question 4.

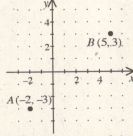

4. Which of the following is the slope of the line perpendicular to the line that passes through points A and B?
   - Ⓐ $\dfrac{7}{6}$
   - Ⓑ $-\dfrac{7}{6}$
   - Ⓒ $\dfrac{6}{7}$
   - Ⓓ $-\dfrac{6}{7}$

Use the figure to answer question 5.

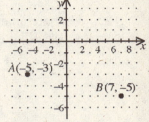

5. What is the distance between points A and B?
   - Ⓐ $\sqrt{37}$
   - Ⓑ $2\sqrt{37}$
   - Ⓒ 37
   - Ⓓ 74

6. Find the slope of the line passing through the points $A(-8, -3)$ and $B(-5, -2)$.
   - Ⓐ $\dfrac{1}{3}$
   - Ⓑ 3
   - Ⓒ $\dfrac{5}{13}$
   - Ⓓ 15

7. Point A has coordinates $(2, -7)$. Which coordinates for point B are such that $\overleftrightarrow{AB}$ is a horizontal line?
   - Ⓐ $(-7, 2)$
   - Ⓑ $(13, 7)$
   - Ⓒ $(-13, -7)$
   - Ⓓ $(-7, -13)$

8. Point A has coordinates $(10, 9)$. Which coordinates for point B are such that $\overleftrightarrow{AB}$ is a vertical line?
   - Ⓐ $(10, -9)$
   - Ⓑ $(-10, -9)$
   - Ⓒ $(9, 10)$
   - Ⓓ $(-9, 10)$

Preparation for the Arkansas End of Course Exam for Geometry

OPEN RESPONSE

A Horizontal and vertical lines are special cases.

1. Sketch a graph of the equation $y = -4$. Why does the graph have zero slope and no x-intercept?

2. What are an equation and graph of a line perpendicular to $y = -4$ that passes through $(3, 0)$? What can you say about the slope of this line?

B A line on a graph has endpoints $(2, 4)$ and $(-6, -1)$.

1. What is the slope of the segment?

2. What is the midpoint of the segment?

52 **Preparation for the Arkansas End of Course Exam for Geometry**

CGT.5.G.2
Write equations of lines in slope-intercept form and use slope to determine parallel and perpendicular lines.

MULTIPLE CHOICE

1. What is the slope of a line perpendicular to the line $3x + 4y = -6$

   Ⓐ $\frac{3}{4}$ Ⓑ $-\frac{3}{4}$
   Ⓒ $\frac{4}{3}$ Ⓓ $-\frac{4}{3}$

Use the figure below to answer question 2.

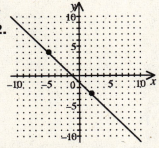

2. The line shown passes through $(-5, 4)$ and $(2, -3)$. What is the equation of the line in slope-intercept form?

   Ⓐ $y = x + 1$ Ⓑ $y = x - 1$
   Ⓒ $y = -x + 1$ Ⓓ $y = -x - 1$

3. Lines m an n lie in the same plane. The slope of line m is $-\frac{5}{3}$ and the slope of line n is $\frac{3}{5}$. How are line m and line n related?

   Ⓐ Line m and line n are coincident.
   Ⓑ Line m does not intersect line n.
   Ⓒ Line m and line n are parallel.
   Ⓓ Line m and line n are perpendicular.

4. What is the relationship between the lines $y = -\frac{1}{3} + 2$ and $y = -\frac{1}{3} - 2$?

   Ⓐ The lines are coincident.
   Ⓑ The lines do not intersect.
   Ⓒ The lines are parallel.
   Ⓓ The lines are perpendicular.

5. What is the slope of a line parallel to the line $5x + 3y = 7$?

   Ⓐ $\frac{3}{5}$ Ⓑ $\frac{5}{3}$
   Ⓒ $-\frac{3}{5}$ Ⓓ $-\frac{5}{3}$

6. Which of the following is a line parallel to $y = \frac{2}{3}x - 7$?

   Ⓐ $y = \frac{3}{2}x + 2$ Ⓑ $y = \frac{2}{3}x + 1$
   Ⓒ $y = -\frac{3}{2}x + 7$ Ⓓ $y = -\frac{2}{3}x - 7$

7. Which equation is of a line parallel to $y = \frac{1}{2}x + 3$ that passes through $(0, 0)$?

   Ⓐ $y = \frac{1}{2}x$
   Ⓑ $y = \frac{1}{2}x + 6$
   Ⓒ $y = 2x$
   Ⓓ $y = \frac{1}{2}x + 3$

8. Which of the following lines is parallel to $4x + y = 7$?

   Ⓐ $x + y = \frac{7}{4}$ Ⓑ $x + 4y = 7$
   Ⓒ $y = -4x + 3$ Ⓓ $y = 4x - 3$

OPEN RESPONSE

A Imagine that you are a highway planner and you want to know the elevation, e, above sea level at many points along a proposed steep linear road grade. You know that the elevation will increase by 800 feet over a road distance, d, of 16,000 feet. Furthermore, the starting elevation is 1200 feet.

1. Beginning at the starting elevation, what is an equation for the line giving the proposed elevation of each point along the road grade?

2. What is the proposed elevation at the 2-mile point?

B A line passes through the point $(-3, 1)$ and is perpendicular to the line $3x - 2y = 7$.

1. What are the slope, y-intercept, and the equation for this line in slope-intercept form?

2. Other than its y-intercept, what is another point through which this line passes?

54 Preparation for the Arkansas End of Course Exam for Geometry

CGT.5.G.3

Determine, given a set of points, the type of figure based on its properties (parallelogram, isosceles triangle, trapezoid).

MULTIPLE CHOICE

1. (2, 3) and (3, 1) are opposite vertices in a parallelogram. If (0, 0) is the third vertex, what is the fourth vertex?

   Ⓐ $\left(\frac{5}{2}, 2\right)$ Ⓑ (−1, 2)

   Ⓒ (5, 4)   Ⓓ (1, −1)

2. The coordinates of quadrilateral PQRS are P(−3, 0), Q(0, 4), R(4, 1), and S(1, −3). Which best describes the quadrilateral?

   Ⓐ a square   Ⓑ a rectangle

   Ⓒ a parallelogram   Ⓓ a rhombus

Use the figure below to answer question 3.

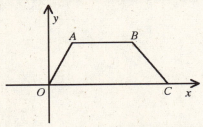

3. What is the midpoint of the midsegment of the trapezoid with vertices O(0, 0), A(4p, 4q), B(4r, 4q), and C(4s, 0)?

   Ⓐ (p + r + s, 2q)

   Ⓑ (2p + 2r, 2q + 2q)

   Ⓒ (r + 2s, 2q)

   Ⓓ (q + r + s, q)

4. Using slope and/or the Distance Formula, what is the most precise name for the figure: A(−4, −4), B(0, −2), C(5, 4), D(1, 2)?

   Ⓐ rectangle   Ⓑ kite

   Ⓒ rhombus   Ⓓ parallelogram

5. What special type of quadrilateral has the vertices M(1, 3), N(5, 3), P(−1, −1), Q(3, −1)?

   Ⓐ kite   Ⓑ trapezoid

   Ⓒ rhombus   Ⓓ rectangle

6. What special type of quadrilateral has the vertices L(−3, 1), M(0, 1), N(−4, −3), P(2, 3)?

   Ⓐ kite   Ⓑ trapezoid

   Ⓒ rhombus   Ⓓ rectangle

Use the figure to answer question 7.

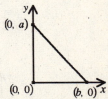

7. A right triangle is placed in a convenient position on the first quadrant of a coordinate plane. If a = 1 and b = 2, what is the distance between (0, a) and (b, 0)?

   Ⓐ $\sqrt{5}$ Ⓑ 5

   Ⓒ $2\sqrt{5}$ Ⓓ 10

Use the figure to answer question 8.

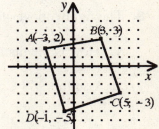

8. What change in vertex location would make ABCD a square?

   Ⓐ move A to (−3, 1)

   Ⓑ move B to (3, 4)

   Ⓒ move C to (5, −4)

   Ⓓ move D to (−1, −4)

Preparation for the Arkansas End of Course Exam for Geometry

OPEN RESPONSE

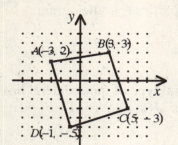

A The figure above shows a quadrilateral.

1. Using the Distance Formula, what are the lengths of AB and DC?

2. Is $ABDC$ a parallelogram? Why or why not?

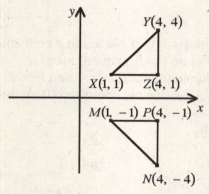

B The figure above shows two triangles.

1. How is the distance between X and Y and between M and N computed?

2. Use the SSS Congruence Postulate to show that $\triangle XYZ \cong \triangle MNP$.

CGT.5.G.4
Write, in standard form, the equation of a circle given a graph on a coordinate plane or the center and radius of a circle.

MULTIPLE CHOICE

1. What is the equation of the circle of radius 4 with its center at the origin?

   A) $x^2 + y^2 = 16$
   B) $\frac{x^2}{8} + \frac{x^2}{8} = 1$
   C) $x^2 + y^2 = 2$
   D) $x^2 + y^2 = 4$

2. What is the equation of the circle with center $(-3, -1)$ and radius of 3?

   A) $(x - 3)^2 + (y - 1)^2 = 3$
   B) $(x + 3)^2 + (y - 1)^2 = 9$
   C) $(x - 3)^2 - (y - 1)^2 = 3$
   D) $(x + 3)^2 + (y + 1)^2 = 9$

Use the figure below to answer question 3.

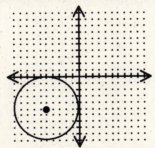

3. A small messenger company can deliver only in a small part of the city. What is an equation for the boundary where the company delivers, and what is its radius?

   A) $(x - 5)^2 + (y - 5)^2 = 50$;
      $r = 25$ blocks
   B) $(x + 5)^2 + (y + 5)^2 = 25$;
      $r = 5$ blocks
   C) $(x + 5)^2 + (y + 5)^2 = 25$;
      $r = 25$ blocks
   D) $(x - 5)^2 + (y - 5)^2 = 50$;
      $r = 5$ blocks

4. The equation of a circle is $(x - 4)^2 + (y + 7)^2 = 36$. What are the coordinates of the center of the circle and the length of the radius?

   A) The center is $(-4, 7)$ and the radius is 6.
   B) The center is $(4, -7)$ and the radius is 6.
   C) The center is $(20, -13)$ and the radius is 36.
   D) The center is $(-20, 13)$ and the radius is 36.

5. The equation of a circle is $(x + 9)^2 + (y + 14)^2 = 16$. What are the coordinates of the center of the circle and the length of the radius?

   A) The center is $(5, 23)$ and the radius is 16.
   B) The center is $(-5, -23)$ and the radius is 16.
   C) The center is $(9, 14)$ and the radius is 4.
   D) The center is $(-9, -14)$ and the radius is 4.

6. The equation of a circle is $(x + 7)^2 + (y + 2)^2 = 16$. Which of these points is inside the circle?

   A) $(7, 1)$
   B) $(-7, 3)$
   C) $(-7, -5)$
   D) $(3, 1)$

7. The equation of a circle is $(x-2)^2 + (y-7)^2 = 16$. Which of these points is inside the circle?

- Ⓐ (2, 1)
- Ⓑ (−7, 3)
- Ⓒ (−7, −5)
- Ⓓ (3, 4)

8. What is the equation of the circle of radius $2\sqrt{2}$ with its center at the origin?

- Ⓐ $x^2 + y^2 = 8$
- Ⓑ $\dfrac{x^2}{8} + \dfrac{y^2}{8} = 1$
- Ⓒ $x^2 + y^2 = 2$
- Ⓓ $x^2 + y^2 = 4$

OPEN RESPONSE

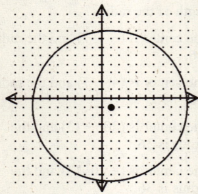

A A certain low-watt radio station is heard in a small part of the city. Each grid unit in the above diagram represents one block.

1. What is an equation for the boundary where the radio station is heard?

2. What is its radius?

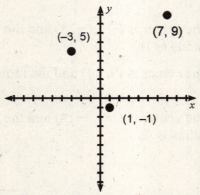

B Consider a coordinate plane and three points, as shown in the figure.

1. How many points are exactly 5 units from (−3, 5) and exactly 6.2 units from (1, −1)?

2. What are the approximate coordinates (to the nearest whole number values) of a single point that is about 5 units from (−3, 5), about 6.2 units from (1, −1), and about 6.2 units from (1, 1)? How can the location of this point be estimated graphically?

58 Preparation for the Arkansas End of Course Exam for Geometry

Name _____ Period _____ Date _____

CGT.5.G.5
Draw and interpret the results of transformations and successive transformations on figures in the coordinate plane
- translations
- reflections
- rotations (90°, 180°, clockwise and counterclockwise about the origin)
- dilations (scale factor)

MULTIPLE CHOICE

1. Which of the following transformations represents an isometry?

   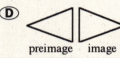

2. Which of the following shows a triangle and its reflection image in the x-axis?

   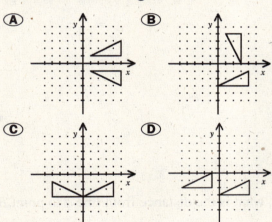

Use the figure to answer question 3.

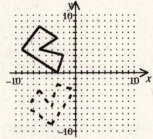

3. Which term best describes the change in position from the solid figure to the dotted figure?
   - Ⓐ rotation
   - Ⓑ transmission
   - Ⓒ translation
   - Ⓓ reflection

4. What does a rigid transformation always map a figure onto?
   - Ⓐ a congruent figure
   - Ⓑ a similar figure
   - Ⓒ itself
   - Ⓓ its mirror image

5. Which picture shows a reflection of the flag?

   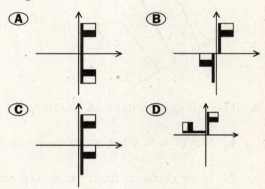

6. Which image does not show a dilation?

   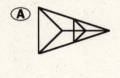
   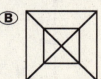
   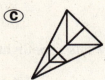

Preparation for the Arkansas End of Course Exam for Geometry

Use the figure below to answer question 7.

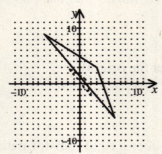

7. The dashed triangle is the image of the solid triangle for a dilation with center at the origin. What is the scale factor?

   Ⓐ 2   Ⓑ $\frac{1}{2}$

   Ⓒ 3   Ⓓ $\frac{1}{3}$

Use the figure below to answer question 8.

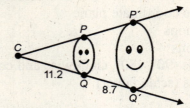

8. To the nearest tenth, what is the scale factor for the dilation shown?

   Ⓐ 2.3   Ⓑ 1.8

   Ⓒ 1.3   Ⓓ 0.8

OPEN RESPONSE

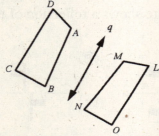

A The reflection image of $\overline{NO}$ in line q is $\overline{BC}$.

1. If $\overline{NO} = 9$, what is the measure of $\overline{BC}$?

2. If the distance from line q to point N is 4, what is the distance from line q to point B?

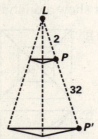

B A lighting designer wants a spotlight to illuminate a triangular section of stage floor.

1. If a screen is placed in front of the light, what is the scale factor of the dilation shown? Hint: L represents the spotlight, P represents the screen, and P' represents the stage floor.

2. What point represents the center of the dilation?

60 Preparation for the Arkansas End of Course Exam for Geometry

Test-Taking Tips for Students

For use before the Arkansas End-of-Course Exam Practice Test

Test-Taking Strategies

To do a task well, you need both competence and confidence. A person playing the guitar for the first time will not sound like a professional, but even a talented guitarist may perform poorly if he or she is tense and worried.

To perform well on a test, you must have the necessary knowledge and problem-solving skills—you must be *competent* in the subject matter. The most important part of test preparation comes from your everyday work during the school year. If you keep up with your homework, pay attention and ask questions in class, and work to understand each new topic as it comes up, you will develop the knowledge you need to perform well on tests. However, there are strategies that will help you apply your knowledge efficiently and avoid obstacles.

You also need to feel *confident* in your test-taking abilities. While success itself is the best confidence booster, there are some simple things you can do that will help you go into a test feeling relaxed and self-assured.

Before the Test

It is difficult to do well on a test when you are tired, hungry, and nervous. The following strategies will help you be at your best when the test begins.

Take one or more practice tests. Taking a practice test is like rehearsing for a play or going to basketball practice. Practice tests help you understand what the real thing will be like and help you identify areas you may need work on.

Get a full night's sleep. Don't stay up too late the night before an important test, even if you are trying to do last-minute "cramming." A good night's sleep will help you concentrate during the test.

Eat a good breakfast. You need a healthy breakfast to be alert and resourceful during a test, especially a long one.

Be on time, and be prepared. It's hard to do your best on a test when you arrive 5 minutes late and without a pencil. (It's also difficult for your classmates to concentrate while you look for an empty desk!) Being on time will give you a few moments to relax before the test begins.

Choose a good seat. Will you be distracted if you sit near a corner or by your friends? Is there a noisy heater along one wall? Select a comfortable place away from distractions.

Be positive. Try not to be intimidated by a test, even one that is especially important. Go into the room ready to show off how much you know.

During the Test

To do your best on a test, you need to work steadily and efficiently. The following ideas will help you keep on track.

Read questions carefully. Before you begin to answer a question, read it completely. Key information may come at the end of the question. Reread the question if you are not sure you understand what it is asking.

Don't read the answers too soon. Whenever possible, answer the question before looking at the answer choices. Even if you cannot come up with the answer right away, your first try may help you understand the question better and eliminate some answers.

Read all choices before marking your answer. Be sure you know all of your options before choosing an answer. If you are having difficulty understanding a question, the answer choices may help you understand what that question is asking.

Pace yourself. Don't try to go through the test as quickly as you can—this can lead to careless mistakes. Work steadily.

Don't get distracted. Resist the temptation to look up every time you hear a rustling paper or a scooting desk. Focus on *your* paper and *your* thought process.

Don't look for patterns. Especially on standardized tests, there is *no way* to tell what answer comes next by looking at previous answers. Don't waste precious time looking for a pattern that isn't there.

Mark your answer sheet carefully. Take a moment to make sure you mark your answer

Preparation for the Arkansas End of Course Exam for Geometry 61

Test-Taking Tips for Students (continued)

in the correct place. This is especially important if you skip one or more problems. When answering multiple-choice tests, be sure to fill in the bubble completely and, if you change an answer, to erase all traces of your old mark.

Check your answers. If you have time, go back and check your answers, filling in answers to any problems you may have skipped. *However* . . .

Be SURE before you change an answer. Your first answer is usually your best answer. Don't change an answer unless you are certain the original answer is incorrect.

If you get stuck, it is important to stay relaxed and confident even if you struggle with some problems. (Even the best test-takers are stumped occasionally!) The following tips will help you work through any temporary setbacks.

Stay calm. Realize that this is only a small part of the test. Don't let a momentary obstacle affect your confidence.

Don't spend too much time on one problem. If you find a problem especially difficult, move on to others that are easier for you. Make the best guess you can and go on, or skip the problem entirely and return to it later if time permits.

Make an educated guess. If you know some of the answer choices are wrong, eliminate those and make the best guess you can from the rest.

> **Example** Find the quotient $-56 \div (-8)$.
>
> **A** -8 **B** -7
>
> **C** 7 **D** 8

There are two parts to this answer, the positive-or-negative sign and the actual number. Since you know the quotient of two negative numbers must *always* be positive, you can eliminate answer choices **A** and **B**.

You may remember $8 \times 8 = 64$, so $7 \times 8 = 56$. Therefore $56 \div 8 = 7$. The correct answer is **C**.

Work backward. If you are having a difficult time with a problem, you may be able to substitute the answers into the problem and see which one is correct.

Which equation is a function rule for the input-output table shown?

> **Example** Which equation is a function rule for the input-output table shown?
>
> | x | 0 | 2 | 4 | 6 | 8 |
> |-----|---|---|---|---|----|
> | y | 2 | 4 | 6 | 8 | 10 |
>
> **A** $y = \frac{x}{2}$ **B** $y = 2x$
>
> **C** $y = x - 2$ **D** $y = x + 2$

To test possible answer choices, use the easiest values from the input-output table. From the table, you know that if $x = 0$ then $y = 2$.

In choice **A**, substitute 0 for x and you find that $y = 0$. So **A** is not correct.

To test choice **B**, again substitute 0 for x and you find that once more $y = 0$. So **B** is not correct.

When you test choice **C** in the same manner, you find that $y = -2$, so **C** is not correct.

In answer choice **D**, when you substitute 0 in place of x, you find that $y = 2$. **D** is the correct answer.

On open-ended problems, be sure your answer covers all that is being asked. Show all of your work and explain your steps or reasoning. Include a diagram if necessary. After you finish your answer, go back and reread the question to make sure you have not left anything out.

After the Test

Reward yourself. If possible, take some time to relax after the test.

Make a plan for the next test. Review what you did before and during the test. Decide which techniques and strategies worked well for you and which ones were not helpful. Think about what you will do differently next time.

Learn from the test. Find out what types of problems caused you the most difficulty and what types you did well on. This will help you prepare for future tests.

Build your confidence for next time. Even if the test did not go well, there are probably some areas where you did succeed. Congratulate yourself on what you did well, and resolve to learn from your mistakes.

Geometry End-of-Course Practice Test

1. Given the conjecture: All animals that swim are fish. What statement is a counterexample to the conjecture?

   Ⓐ Mice are not fish and mice do not swim.

   Ⓑ Whales are not fish and whales can swim.

   Ⓒ Fish are not mammals and mammals do not swim.

   Ⓓ Flathead catfish are fish and flathead catfish can swim.

2. Month after month, the moon is observed to go through a complete set of phases from full to new and back to full again every 29.5 days. Through what type of reasoning can the conclusion that the period of the moon's orbit around Earth is 29.5 days be drawn?

   Ⓐ counterexample

   Ⓑ deductive reasoning

   Ⓒ syllogism

   Ⓓ inductive reasoning

Use the figure to answer question 3.

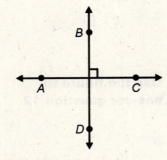

3. Which description best explains what is shown in the figure?

   Ⓐ Two rays that are perpendicular

   Ⓑ Two lines that are perpendicular

   Ⓒ $AC = BD$

   Ⓓ A straight angle

Use the figure below to answer question 4.

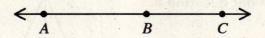

4. If $BC = 18$ and $AC = 37$, what is the length of $\overline{AB}$?

   Ⓐ 55 Ⓑ 37

   Ⓒ 19 Ⓓ 18

5. Under what condition do distinct points A, B, and C lie in more than one plane?

   Ⓐ A, B, and C are collinear

   Ⓑ $BC \perp AC$

   Ⓒ $AB \perp AC$

   Ⓓ $\triangle ABC$ is equilateral

Use the sequence below to answer question 6.

$$1;\ 7;\ 17;\ 31;\ ...$$

6. What is the next number in the sequence?

   Ⓐ 47 Ⓑ 49

   Ⓒ 51 Ⓓ 63

Use the figure below to answer question 7.

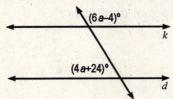

7. In the diagram, $k \parallel d$ with the angle measures indicated. What is the value of a?

   Ⓐ 18 Ⓑ 16

   Ⓒ 14 Ⓓ 12

Preparation for the Arkansas End of Course Exam for Geometry

Geometry End-of-Course Practice Test

Use the figure to answer question 8.

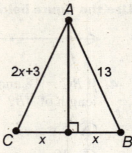

8. What property best describes triangle △ABC and what is the value of x?

   Ⓐ △ABC is isosceles and x = 5
   Ⓑ △ABC is equilateral and x = 5
   Ⓒ △ABC is isosceles and x = 6.5
   Ⓓ △ABC is equilateral and x = 6.5

Use the figure to answer question 9.

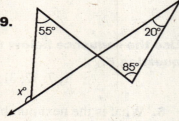

9. In the figure, what is the value of x?

   Ⓐ 110°
   Ⓑ 120°
   Ⓒ 130°
   Ⓓ cannot determine

Use the figure below to answer question 10.

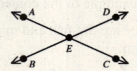

10. If $m\angle AED = 140°$, which of the following statements is false?

    Ⓐ ∠BEC and ∠CED are adjacent angles
    Ⓑ ∠AEB and ∠DEC are vertical angles
    Ⓒ $m\angle BEC = 140°$
    Ⓓ $m\angle AEB = 140°$

Use the figure to answer question 11.

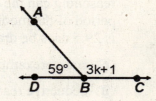

11. ∠ABC and ∠ABD are a linear pair of angles. What is the value of k?

    Ⓐ −10   Ⓑ 10
    Ⓒ 19   Ⓓ 40

Use the figure to answer question 12.

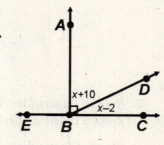

12. If $\overline{AB} \perp \overline{EC}$, what is the value of x?

    Ⓐ 80   Ⓑ 41
    Ⓒ 40   Ⓓ 36

64 Preparation for the Arkansas End of Course Exam for Geometry

Geometry End-of-Course Practice Test

Use the figure below to answer question 13.

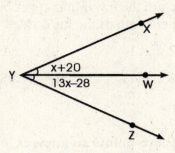

13. In the diagram, $\overrightarrow{YW}$ bisects $\angle XYZ$ with the angle measures indicated. What is the value of x?

    Ⓐ 2   Ⓑ 3
    Ⓒ 4   Ⓓ 6

Use the table below to answer question 14.

$\angle 1$ and $\angle 2$ are both complementary to $\angle 3$	Given
$\angle 1$ and $\angle 2$ are congruent	?

14. What is the theorem or postulate that provides the best justification for the second step of the above argument?

    Ⓐ Congruent Supplements Theorem
    Ⓑ Vertical Angles Theorem
    Ⓒ Congruent Complements Theorem
    Ⓓ Linear Pair Postulate

15. Vertical angles have equal measures. If $\angle A$ has measure 47° and is vertical to $\angle C$, what conclusion may be drawn?

    Ⓐ $\angle C$ has measure 180°
    Ⓑ The sum $m\angle C + m\angle A$ is 90°
    Ⓒ $\angle C$ is complimentary to a 47° angle
    Ⓓ $\angle C$ has measure 47°

16. Let $\angle 1$ and $\angle 2$ be vertical angles and let $\angle 1$ and $\angle 3$ be complimentary angles. If $m\angle 2 = 72°$ then what is $m\angle 3$?

    Ⓐ 18°   Ⓑ 28°
    Ⓒ 72°   Ⓓ 108°

Use the figure below to answer question 17.

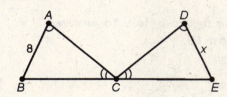

17. Given that $\angle A \cong \angle D$, $\angle ACB \cong \angle DCE$, and C is the midpoint of $\overline{BE}$, which postulate or theorem allows you to determine the value of x?

    Ⓐ SSS Congruence Postulate
    Ⓑ AAS Congruence Theorem
    Ⓒ ASA Congruence Postulate
    Ⓓ SAS Congruence Postulate

Geometry End-of-Course Practice Test

Use the figure to answer question 18.

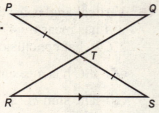

18. Given $\overline{PQ} \parallel \overline{RS}$ and $PT = TS$, which theorem or theorems allow you to state that $\angle QPS \cong \angle TSR$ and $\angle PTQ \cong \angle RTS$ so that the ASA Congruence Postulate proves $\triangle PQT \cong \triangle RST$?

   A. the Alternate Interior Angles theorem and the Vertical Angles theorem
   B. the Alternate Exterior Angles theorem and the Vertical Angles theorem
   C. the Hinge Theorem
   D. the Base Angles Theorem

Use the figure below to answer question 19.

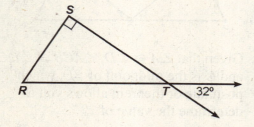

19. What is the measure of $\angle SRT$?

   A. 32°
   B. 45°
   C. 58°
   D. 72°

20. Which group of three side lengths will *not* allow you to construct a triangle?

   A. 2, 5, and 8
   B. 4, 9, and 11
   C. 6, 8, and 10
   D. 7, 14, and 20

21. One side of a triangle has length 8 units and another side has length 11 units. What are the lower and upper bounds for the length of the third side?

   A. 3 and 11
   B. 3 and 19
   C. 8 and 11
   D. 11 and 19

Use the figure below to answer question 22.

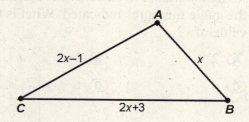

22. Which inequality is a solution for all possible values of x?

   A. $x < \frac{3}{2}$
   B. $x > 0$
   C. $x > \frac{1}{2}$
   D. $x > 4$

Use the figure below to answer question 23.

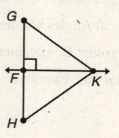

23. If $\overleftrightarrow{KF}$ is the perpendicular bisector of $\overline{GH}$, then which angle is congruent to $\angle FKG$?

   A. $\angle KHF$
   B. $\angle KFH$
   C. $\angle FKH$
   D. $\angle KGF$

Geometry End-of-Course Practice Test

Use the figure below to answer question 24.

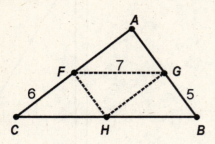

24. For the triangle shown, $AF = FC = 6$, $AG = GB = 5$, $CH = HB$, and $FG = 7$. What is the length CB?

   Ⓐ 14 Ⓑ 12
   Ⓒ 11 Ⓓ 10

25. How long is a ladder that reaches from the top of a 25-ft wall to a point 12 ft from the base of the wall?

   Ⓐ 13 ft Ⓑ $\sqrt{481}$ ft
   Ⓒ $\sqrt{769}$ ft Ⓓ 37 ft

26. A radio station wants to construct a new antenna. The antenna must be supported by three separate cables. Each cable must be attached half-way from the base to the top of the antenna, and to points on the flat roof of the building that must be at least 12 feet from the base of the antenna. A total usable length of 39 feet of cable is all that is available. What is the tallest antenna that can be supported with the available cable?

   Ⓐ 5 ft Ⓑ 10 ft
   Ⓒ 12 ft Ⓓ 13 ft

Use the figure below to answer question 27.

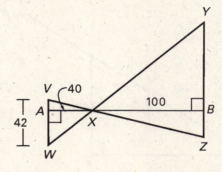

27. In the diagram, $VW = 42$, $AX = 40$, and $XB = 100$. What is the length YZ?

   Ⓐ 140 Ⓑ 105
   Ⓒ 82 Ⓓ 60

28. A square has a diagonal with length $9\sqrt{2}$. What is the length of a side of the square?

   Ⓐ 18 Ⓑ $9\sqrt{2}$
   Ⓒ 9 Ⓓ $\sqrt{2}$

29. The hypotenuse of a $30° - 60° - 90°$ triangle is 10 feet long. What is the perimeter of the triangle?

   Ⓐ $15 + 10\sqrt{3}$ ft
   Ⓑ $15 + 5\sqrt{3}$ ft
   Ⓒ $10 + 5\sqrt{3}$ ft
   Ⓓ $5 + 10\sqrt{3}$ ft

Name _____ Period _____ Date _____

Geometry End-of-Course Practice Test

Use the figure below to answer question 30.

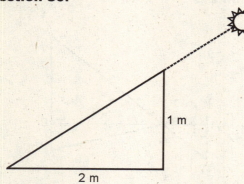

30. Jared wants to measure the angle of elevation of the sun above the horizon at a certain time. He notes that an upright 1 meter stick casts a shadow that is 2 meters long. To the nearest degree, what should Jared record as the approximate angle of elevation of the sun?

   Ⓐ 27° Ⓑ 30°
   Ⓒ 60° Ⓓ 63°

Use the figure below to answer question 31.

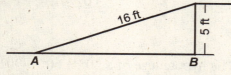

31. The figure shows a 16 ft ramp leading up to a loading dock that forms an angle with the ground. The loading dock height is 5 ft. What is the approximate distance to the nearest hundredth foot from point A to point B along the ground under the ramp and the approximate angle to the nearest degree that the ramp makes with the ground?

   Ⓐ 16.76 feet and 18°
   Ⓑ 16.76 feet and 15°
   Ⓒ 15.20 feet and 18°
   Ⓓ 15.20 feet and 15°

Use the figure to answer question 32.

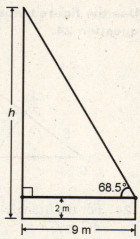

32. A surveyor using a transit mounted 2 meters high and 9 meters from the base of a mast measures a 68.5° angle of elevation to the top of a mast as shown in the figure. What is the height, h, of the mast to the nearest centimeter?

   Ⓐ $h = 22.85$ m Ⓑ $h = 24.85$ m
   Ⓒ $h = 26.55$ m Ⓓ $h = 28.55$ m

33. M is the midpoint of $\overline{AB}$ and Q is the midpoint of $\overline{MB}$. If a point of $\overline{AB}$ is picked at random, what is the probability that the point is on $\overline{AQ}$?

   Ⓐ 1 Ⓑ $\frac{3}{4}$
   Ⓒ $\frac{1}{2}$ Ⓓ $\frac{1}{4}$

Use the figure below to answer question 34.

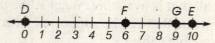

34. What is the probability that a point chosen at random on $\overline{DE}$ is on $\overline{DF}$ or $\overline{GE}$?

   Ⓐ 100% Ⓑ 70%
   Ⓒ 30% Ⓓ 0%?

Geometry End-of-Course Practice Test

Use the figure below to answer question 35.

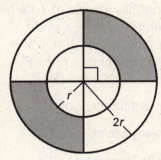

35. If a dart is thrown so that it sticks at a random point within the target shown, what is the probability it is *not* in a gray area?

   Ⓐ $\frac{1}{4}$ Ⓑ $\frac{3}{8}$
   Ⓒ $\frac{1}{2}$ Ⓓ $\frac{5}{8}$

36. An aquarium in a restaurant is a rectangular prism and measures 3 feet by 4.5 feet by 6 feet. What is the volume of the aquarium?

   Ⓐ 81 cubic feet   Ⓑ 64 cubic feet
   Ⓒ 49 cubic feet   Ⓓ 36 cubic feet

Use the figure to answer question 37.

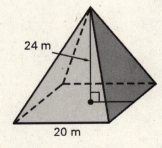

37. What is the volume of the pyramid?

   Ⓐ 480 m³   Ⓑ 4800 m³
   Ⓒ 3200 m³   Ⓓ 9600 m³

38. What happens to the volume of a rectangular prism if both its length and its height are doubled while its width is halved?

   Ⓐ The volume cannot be determined.
   Ⓑ The volume is doubled.
   Ⓒ The volume is unchanged.
   Ⓓ The volume is multiplied by a factor of $\frac{1}{2}$.

39. A solid steel cylinder weighs 18 lbs. How much does another such cylinder weigh if its radius is one-third that of the 18 lb cylinder?

   Ⓐ 9 lb   Ⓑ 6 lb
   Ⓒ 3 lb   Ⓓ 2 lb

40. Two spherical tanks were constructed from shells of sheet metal. One tank holds 8 times more water than the other. How many times more area of sheet metal were used in the construction of the larger tank over that used in the smaller tank?

   Ⓐ 8   Ⓑ 4
   Ⓒ 2   Ⓓ $\sqrt[3]{4}$

Preparation for the Arkansas End of Course Exam for Geometry

Geometry End-of-Course Practice Test

Use the figure to answer question 41.

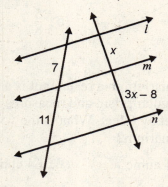

41. What is the scale factor for the dilation shown?

- (A) $\frac{21}{12}$
- (B) 2
- (C) $\frac{21}{9}$
- (D) $\frac{4}{3}$

42. The perimeter of equilateral triangle *ABC* is 18. Triangle *ABC* is similar to triangle *EFG* and the scale factor is 3. What is the length *EF*?

- (A) 6
- (B) 4
- (C) 3
- (D) 2

Use the figure below to answer question 43.

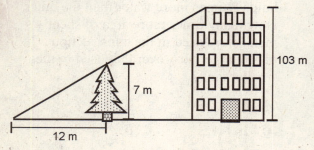

43. Josh wants to find the distance from a 7 m tree to a tall building. The tree is exactly 12 m in front of him, and the building is known to be 103 m in height. He sights the top of the building just at the top of the tree. To the nearest meter, what is the approximate distance from the tree to the building?

- (A) 84 m
- (B) 177 m
- (C) 165 m
- (D) 153 m

44. You want to use a pantograph to make a re-sized copy of a blueprint. The original blueprint has a scale of 1 inch = 10 feet. The copy is to have a scale of 1 inch = 2 feet. Will this copy be an enlargement or a reduction, and what is the scale factor?

- (A) enlargement, 1 to 4
- (B) enlargement, 1 to 5
- (C) reduction, 4 to 1
- (D) reduction, 5 to 1

Use the figure below to answer question 45.

45. Given $l \parallel m \parallel n$, what is the value of *x*?

- (A) 3.5
- (B) 4.9
- (C) 5.6
- (D) 7

70 Preparation for the Arkansas End of Course Exam for Geometry

Geometry End-of-Course Practice Test

Use the figure below to answer question 46.

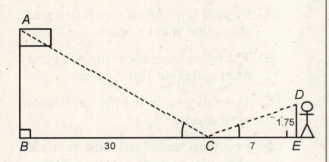

46. Lashauna wanted to measure the height of her school's flagpole. She placed a mirror on the ground 30 meters from the flagpole, then walked backwards until she was able to see the top of the pole in the mirror. She observed the mirror from a point 1.75 m above the ground, and she was 7 m from the mirror. What is the height of the flagpole?

   Ⓐ 23 m   Ⓑ 17 m
   Ⓒ 7.5 m   Ⓓ 4.5 m

Use the figure below to answer question 47.

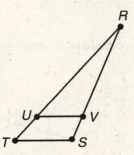

47. Given that, $RU = 3UT$ and $RV = 3VS$, what must be true about the relationship between $\overline{UV}$ and $\overline{TS}$?

   Ⓐ $UV = TS$ Ⓑ $UV > TS$
   Ⓒ $\overline{UV} \parallel \overline{TS}$ Ⓓ $\overline{UV} \perp \overline{TS}$

Use the figure below to answer question 48.

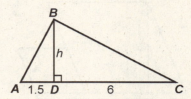

48. Right triangle ABC has altitude $\overline{BD}$ of length h to hypotenuse $\overline{AC}$. If $AD = 1.5$ and $DC = 6$, what is the value of h?

   Ⓐ 3   Ⓑ 4
   Ⓒ 4.5   Ⓓ 6

Use the figure below to answer question 49.

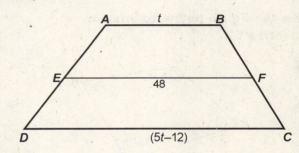

49. Trapezoid $ABCD$ has median $\overline{EF}$. What is the value of t?

   Ⓐ 8   Ⓑ 12
   Ⓒ 18   Ⓓ 30

50. Which statement is *not* always true?

   Ⓐ A square is a rhombus.
   Ⓑ A trapezoid does not have two pairs of parallel sides.
   Ⓒ A rhombus has diagonals of equal length.
   Ⓓ A parallelogram has diagonals that bisect each other.

Geometry End-of-Course Practice Test

Use the figure below to answer question 51.

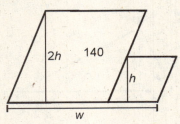

51. The quadrilaterals sharing one side in the figure are both rhombuses. The larger one has area 140 square units. If $h = 5$ units, what is the length w?

    Ⓐ 35 units Ⓑ 21 units
    Ⓒ 14 units Ⓓ 7 units

Use the figure below to answer question 52.

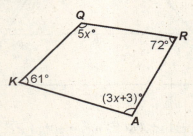

52. Quadrilateral *KQRA* has interior angles as shown. What is the value of x?

    Ⓐ 133 Ⓑ 65
    Ⓒ 28   Ⓓ 20

53. Which of the following polygons can not form a regular tessellation?

    Ⓐ regular hexagon
    Ⓑ regular pentagon
    Ⓒ square
    Ⓓ equilateral triangle

54. Which of the following is a rule for regular tessellations?

    Ⓐ Regular tessellations must cover a shape that is not a plane.
    Ⓑ The interior angles of the polygons must add up to 180 degrees
    Ⓒ The polygons in regular tessellations must overlap
    Ⓓ Regular tessellations must be made of regular polygons that are all the same.

55. What is the surface area of a regular tetrahedron of side length 10 cm?

    Ⓐ $100\sqrt{3}$ cm^2 Ⓑ $10\sqrt{30}$ cm^2
    Ⓒ $4\sqrt{3}$ cm^2 Ⓓ $3\sqrt{3}$ cm^2

56. Which of the following polygons can always be used to form a two-dimensional net for a platonic solid?

    Ⓐ kite
    Ⓑ isosceles triangle
    Ⓒ trapezoid
    Ⓓ equilateral triangle

Use the figure below to answer question 57.

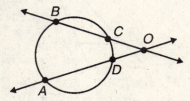

Not drawn to scale

57. Given that $m\widehat{AB} = 63°$, $m\widehat{CD} = 15°$, what is $m\angle AOB$?

    Ⓐ 24° Ⓑ 39°
    Ⓒ 48° Ⓓ 78°

Geometry End-of-Course Practice Test

Use the figure below to answer question 58.

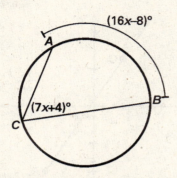

58. In the figure, $m\overset{\frown}{AB}$ and $m\angle ACB$ are related as shown. What is the value of x?

   Ⓐ 6 Ⓑ 8
   Ⓒ 10 Ⓓ 12

Use the figure below to answer question 59.

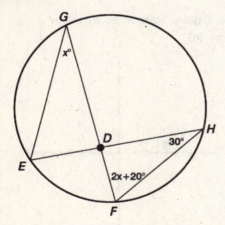

59. What are $m\angle EGD$ and $m\angle EDG$ in the inscribed figure?

   Ⓐ 30° and 50° Ⓑ 60° and 50°
   Ⓒ 30° and 70° Ⓓ 60° and 70°

Use the figure below to answer question 60.

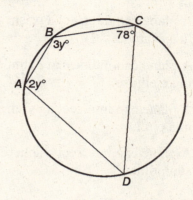

60. Quadrilateral $ABCD$ is inscribed in the circle. What is the measure of $\angle ADC$?

   Ⓐ 23° Ⓑ 27°
   Ⓒ 32° Ⓓ 36°

Use the figures below to answer question 61.

Front view	Top view	Side view

61. Which solid has the three views shown in the figures?

   Ⓐ 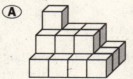 Ⓑ

   Ⓒ 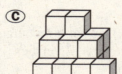 Ⓓ

Preparation for the Arkansas End of Course Exam for Geometry

Geometry End-of-Course Practice Test

62. Which of the following statements is false?

    A. A plane can intersect a prism in a triangle.

    B. A plane can intersect a cylinder in an ellipse.

    C. A plane can intersect a pyramid in a circle.

    D. A plane can intersect a sphere at a point.

63. Which of the following best describes a possible cross section of an doughnut?

    A. pentagon B. circle
    C. trapezoid D. prism

64. Which of the following equations state and verify Euler's theorem for the number of faces (F), vertices (V), and edges (E) of a rectangular prism?

    A. $F + V = E + 2$, so for a rectangular prism, $6 + 8 = 12 + 2$ verifies Euler's theorem

    B. $F + V = E + 2$, so for a rectangular prism, $6 + 6 = 10 + 2$ verifies Euler's theorem

    C. $F + E = V + 2$, so for a rectangular prism, $6 + 4 = 8 + 2$ verifies Euler's theorem

    D. $F + E = V + 2$, so for a rectangular prism, $8 + 6 = 12 + 2$ verifies Euler's theorem

Use the figure below to answer question 65.

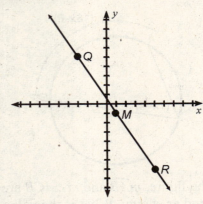

65. The midpoint of $\overline{QR}$ is $M(-1, -1)$. One endpoint is $Q(-3, 5)$. What are the coordinates of the other endpoint?

    A. $(-5, 7)$ B. $(5, -7)$
    C. $(7, -5)$ D. $(-7, -5)$

Use the figure below to answer question 66.

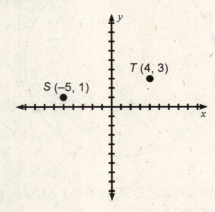

66. What is the approximate distance (to the nearest hundredth) between points S and T?

    A. 6.45 B. 7.72
    C. 9.21 D. 13.00

Geometry End-of-Course Practice Test

Use the figure below to answer question 67.

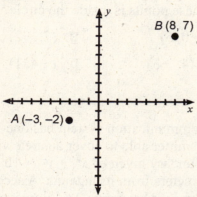

67. What is the slope of the line perpendicular to the line that passes through points A and B?

   Ⓐ $-\dfrac{11}{9}$ Ⓑ $\dfrac{11}{9}$

   Ⓒ $-\dfrac{11}{5}$ Ⓓ $\dfrac{5}{11}$

68. Point Z has coordinates $(-9, 13)$. Which coordinates for point Y are such that $\overleftrightarrow{YZ}$ is a horizontal line?

   Ⓐ $(-9, -9)$ Ⓑ $(13, 9)$

   Ⓒ $(-13, -9)$ Ⓓ $(13, 13)$

69. What is the slope of a line perpendicular to the line $-9x + 5y = -6$

   Ⓐ $-\dfrac{5}{9}$ Ⓑ $-\dfrac{9}{5}$

   Ⓒ $\dfrac{5}{9}$ Ⓓ $\dfrac{5}{6}$

70. Which of the following is a line parallel to $y = -\dfrac{4}{3}x - 7$ that passes through $(0, -1)$?

   Ⓐ $y = -\dfrac{4}{3}x$ Ⓑ $y = -\dfrac{4}{3}x - 1$

   Ⓒ $y = \dfrac{4}{3}x + 1$ Ⓓ $y = \dfrac{3}{4}x - 1$

Use the figure below to answer question 71.

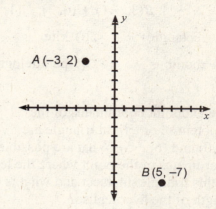

71. What is an equation of the line passing through points A and B?

   Ⓐ $9x + 8y = -11$

   Ⓑ $8x + 9y = 11$

   Ⓒ $9x - 8y = -11$

   Ⓓ $-9x + 8y = 11$

Use the figure below to answer question 72.

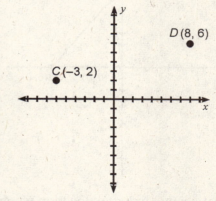

72. What is the equation in slope-intercept form of the line passing through points C and D?

   Ⓐ $-4x + 11y = 34$ Ⓑ $y = \dfrac{4}{11}x + \dfrac{34}{11}$

   Ⓒ $y = 11x + 4$ Ⓓ $y = \dfrac{11}{4}x + \dfrac{34}{4}$

Preparation for the Arkansas End of Course Exam for Geometry

Geometry End-of-Course Practice Test

73. What is the most precise name for quadrilateral ABCD with coordinates $A(-2, -1), B(3, -1), C(6, 3), D(1, 3)$?

- Ⓐ rectangle
- Ⓑ kite
- Ⓒ rhombus
- Ⓓ parallelogram

74. The endpoint coordinates of the hypotenuse of a right triangle are $(1, 0)$ and $(6, -5)$. What are possible coordinates of the point where the legs of this triangle intersect and what is the length of the hypotenuse?

- Ⓐ $(6, 0)$ and $5\sqrt{3}$
- Ⓑ $(6, 0)$ and $5\sqrt{2}$
- Ⓒ $(1, -5)$ and $5\sqrt{3}$
- Ⓓ $(1, 5)$ and $5\sqrt{2}$

Use the figure below to answer question 75.

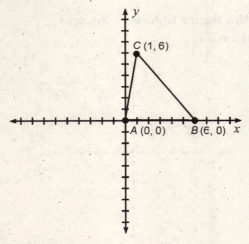

75. What change in vertex location would make ABC an equilateral triangle?

- Ⓐ move A to $(-1, -1)$
- Ⓑ move C to $(3, \sqrt{3})$
- Ⓒ move C to $(3, 3)$
- Ⓓ move C to $(3, 3\sqrt{3})$

76. The equation of a circle is $(x - 1)^2 + (y + 2)^2 = 25$. Which of these points is inside the circle?

- Ⓐ $(0, 5)$
- Ⓑ $(7, -2)$
- Ⓒ $(4, -3)$
- Ⓓ $(-4, 1)$

77. A communication system has one transmitter able to cover an area within a boundary given by $x^2 + y^2 = 16$ kilometers from its antenna. A second transmitter has range 2.5 kilometers. Placement of the second transmitter at which of these coordinates would allow it to cover the point at $(4, 4)$, yet not overlap coverage of the first transmitter?

- Ⓐ $(3, 3)$
- Ⓑ $(4, 4)$
- Ⓒ $(-3, 6)$
- Ⓓ $(3, 6)$

78. Which of the following shows a triangle and its image after a translation $(x, y) \rightarrow (x + 5, y - 1)$.

Ⓐ 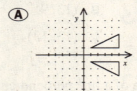   Ⓑ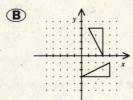

Ⓒ 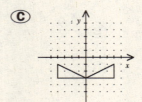   Ⓓ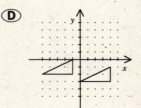

Geometry End-of-Course Practice Test

Use the figure to answer question 79.

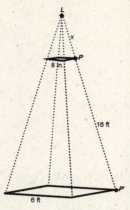

79. A lighting designer wants to illuminate a rectangular area of floor (at P') that is 6 ft wide using a spotlight (at L) and similar rectangular screen (at P). The screen has a rectangular opening that is 8 inches wide and is located 16 ft from the floor along a line to the corner of the illuminated area as shown in the figure. What should be the distance x in order to obtain this dilation of illuminated area from screen to floor?

Ⓐ $1\frac{7}{9}$ ft   Ⓑ 2 ft

Ⓒ $2\frac{7}{9}$ ft   Ⓓ 3 ft

Use the figure to answer question 80.

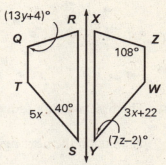

80. The transformation shown in the figure is an isometry. What are the values of the variables?

Ⓐ $x = 8, y = 2, z = 5$

Ⓑ $x = -22, y = 2, z = 3$

Ⓒ $x = 11, y = -8, z = 11$

Ⓓ $x = 11, y = 8, z = 6$

Name _____ Period _____ Date _____

Geometry Open-Response Item A

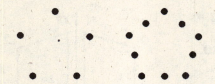

A The first two of a sequence of figures are shown above.

1. Sketch the next figure.

2. What is an expression for the number of dots in the *n*th figure?

BE SURE TO LABEL YOUR RESPONSES (1) AND (2).

Geometry Open-Response Item B

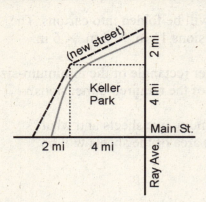

B The City Commission wants to construct a new street in two segments so that it skirts Keller Park while connecting Main Street and Ray Avenue as shown in the diagram. The construction cost for this road has been estimated at $135 per linear foot. (1 mile = 5280 ft)

1. For how many miles of roadway (rounding up to the next 0.01 mi) must the Commission budget in order to build the new street?

2. What is the estimated cost for constructing the new street?

BE SURE TO LABEL YOUR RESPONSES (1) AND (2).

Name _____ **Period** _____ **Date** _____

Geometry Open-Response Item C

C A die is to be made for cutting flat cardboard sheets that will be folded into cartons. The cartons are to be rectangular prisms and must have dimensions 16 in. × 8 in. × 6 in.

1. Make a sketch of the shape of the die showing the outer rectangle of the minimum-size sheet from which the cartons can be cut. What are all of the required dimensions?

2. What shape and dimensions are required for the minimum-size sheets and what approximate percentage (to the nearest percent) of the area of the sheets will be discarded in the manufacture of the cartons?

BE SURE TO LABEL YOUR RESPONSES (1) AND (2).

Geometry Open-Response Item D

Front view

Side view

Top view

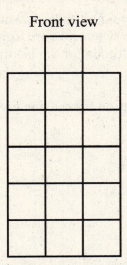
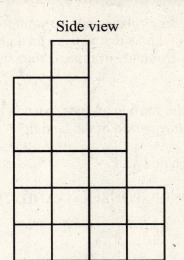
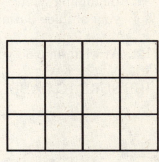

D A model of a building design is to be constructed from cubes. The figures show orthographic projections of the design.

1. Show how to compute the required volume (in cubes) of the design. How many total cubes will be required to construct the model of the building?

2. On the grid of dots below, make an isometric drawing of the building.

BE SURE TO LABEL YOUR RESPONSES (1) AND (2).

Name	Period	Date

Geometry Open-Response Item E

E Imagine that you are piloting an airplane and you want to know your altitude, h, while descending into an airport. You know that you are on a glide path where you are losing altitude at a rate of 500 feet per minute of time, t. Your starting altitude for the landing was 5750 feet.

1. Beginning with $t = 0$ at the starting altitude, what is the equation for the line giving your altitude during the time period of the landing?

2. At what time do you touch down?

BE SURE TO LABEL YOUR RESPONSES (1) AND (2).

82 **Preparation for the Arkansas End of Course Exam for Geometry**

Name _____ **Period** _____ **Date** _____

Geometry Open-Response Item F

F Suppose you are a landscape designer and you want to fit a garden space next to one side of a patio. The garden must fit in a rectangular area that is 15 feet deep from the patio and 30 feet wide on the side of the patio. The garden is to have a minimum 5-foot-wide walkway around its perimeter. The garden will require topsoil fill to a depth of 1 foot.

1. What are two possible shapes for the garden, one semi-circular and the other rectangular? Make two sketches to illustrate the possible designs.

2. Which garden shape would require more topsoil fill? Compute to the nearest tenth the required volume of fill for each shape in cubic yards.

BE SURE TO LABEL YOUR RESPONSES (1) AND (2).

Preparation for the Arkansas End of Course Exam for Geometry **83**

Arkansas Learning Expectations	End-of-Course Practice Test Items		Remediation	
			McDougal Littell Geometry	McDougal Littell Geometry Concepts & Skills
LG.1.G.1 Define, compare and contrast inductive reasoning and deductive reasoning for making predictions based on real world situations: • venn diagrams • matrix logic • conditional statements (statement, inverse, converse, and contrapositive)	ITEM 1, 2 CORRECT ___/2		1.1 2.1 2.3	1.2 2.5 3.5
LG.1.G.2 Represent points, lines, and planes pictorially with proper identification, as well as basic concepts derived from these undefined terms, such as segments, rays, and angles	ITEM 3, 4, 5 CORRECT ___/3		1.2 1.3 1.4	1.3 1.4 1.5 1.6
LG.1.G.3 Describe relationships derived from geometric figures or figural patterns	ITEM 6, 7, 8, 9, A CORRECT ___/5		9.4	6.1 6.2 6.3 6.4 6.5 6.6 8.5
LG.1.G.4 Apply, with and without appropriate technology, definitions, theorems, properties, and postulates related to such topics as complementary, supplementary, vertical angles, linear pairs, and angles formed by perpendicular lines	ITEM 10, 11, 12, 15, 16 CORRECT ___/5		1.6 2.2 2.6	2.3 2.4 3.2 3.3
LG.1.G.5 Explore, with and without appropriate technology, the relationship between angles formed by two lines cut by a transversal to justify when lines are parallel	ITEM 7 CORRECT ___/1		3.3 3.4 3.5	3.5 3.6
LG.1.G.6 Give justification for conclusions reached by deductive reasoning	ITEM 13, 14 CORRECT ___/2		2.5 2.6 3.2 3.4 4.3 4.4 4.7 6.3	5.2 5.3
T.2.G.1 Apply congruence (SSS . . .) and similarity (AA . . .) correspondences and properties of figures to find missing parts of geometric figures and provide logical justification	ITEM 17, 18, 19, 27 CORRECT ___/4		4.3 4.4 4.5 8.3 8.4 8.5 8.6	5.1 5.2 5.3 5.4 5.5 7.2 7.3 7.4 7.5

Preparation for the Arkansas End of Course Exam for Geometry

Arkansas Learning Expectations	End-of-Course Practice Test Items		Remediation	
			McDougal Littell Geometry	McDougal Littell Geometry Concepts & Skills
T.2.G.2 Investigate the measures of segments to determine the existence of triangles (triangle inequality theorem)	ITEM	20, 21, 22	5.5 9.3	4.7
	CORRECT	___/3		
T.2.G.3 Identify and use the special segments of triangles (altitude, median, angle bisector, perpendicular bisector, and midsegment) to solve problems	ITEM	23, 24	5.2 5.3 5.4	4.6 5.6 7.5
	CORRECT	___/2		
T.2.G.4 Apply the Pythagorean Theorem and its converse in solving practical problems	ITEM	25, 26, B	9.2 9.3	4.4 4.5
	CORRECT	___/3		
T.2.G.5 Use the special right triangle relationships (30°-60°-90° and 45°-45°-90°) to solve problems	ITEM	28, 29	9.4	10.2 10.3
	CORRECT	___/2		
T.2.G.6 Use trigonometric ratios (sine, cosine, tangent) to determine lengths of sides and measures of angles in right triangles including angles of elevation and angles of depression	ITEM	30, 31, 32	9.5 9.6	10.4 10.5 10.6
	CORRECT	___/3		
M.3.G.1 Calculate probabilities arising in geometric contexts (Ex. Find the probability of hitting a particular ring on a dartboard.)	ITEM	33, 34, 35	11.6	pp. 713–714
	CORRECT	___/3		
M.3.G.2 Apply, using appropriate units, appropriate formulas (area, perimeter, surface area, volume) to solve application problems involving polygons, prisms, pyramids, cones, cylinders, spheres as well as composite figures, expressing solutions in both exact and approximate forms	ITEM	36, 37, C	11.2 12.2 12.3 12.4 12.5 12.6	7.2 8.3 8.4 8.5 8.6 9.2 9.3 9.4 9.5 9.6
	CORRECT	___/3		

86 **Preparation for the Arkansas End of Course Exam for Geometry**

Arkansas Learning Expectations	End-of-Course Practice Test Items	Remediation	
		McDougal Littell Geometry	McDougal Littell Geometry Concepts & Skills
M.3.G.3 Relate changes in the measurement of one attribute of an object to changes in other attributes (Ex. How does changing the radius or height of a cylinder affect its surface area or volume?)	ITEM 38, 39, 40, F CORRECT ___/4	12.2 12.3	9.2 9.3 9.5 9.6
M.3.G.4 Use (given similar geometric objects) proportional reasoning to solve practical problems (including scale drawings)	ITEM 41, 42, 43, 44, 46, 48 CORRECT ___/6	8.3 8.4 8.5 8.6 8.7 11.3	7.2 7.3 7.4 7.6
M.3.G.5 Use properties of parallel lines and proportional reasoning to find the lengths of segments	ITEM 45, 47 CORRECT ___/2	8.6	7.1 7.2 7.3 7.5
R.4.G.1 Explore and verify the properties of quadrilaterals	ITEM 49, 50, 51 CORRECT ___/3	6.1 6.2 6.3 6.4 6.5 6.6	6.1 6.2 6.3 6.4 6.5 6.6
R.4.G.2 Solve problems using properties of polygons: • sum of the measures of the interior angles of a polygon • interior and exterior angle measure of a regular polygon or irregular polygon • number of sides or angles of a polygon	ITEM 52 CORRECT ___/1	6.1 6.2 6.5	8.2
R.4.G.3 Identify and explain why figures tessellate	ITEM 53, 54 CORRECT ___/2	Project for Chapters 6 and 7 pp. 452–453	Project for Chapters 5 and 6 pp. 352–353
R.4.G.4 Identify the attributes of the five Platonic Solids	ITEM 55, 56, 64 CORRECT ___/3	12.1	9.1 9.3
R.4.G.5 Investigate and use the properties of angles (central and inscribed) arcs, chords, tangents, and secants to solve problems involving circles	ITEM 57, 58 CORRECT ___/2	10.1 10.2 10.3 10.4	11.1 11.2 11.3 11.4 11.5 11.6

Copyright © by McDougal Littell, a division of Houghton Mifflin Company.

Preparation for the Arkansas End of Course Exam for Geometry 87

Arkansas Learning Expectations	End-of-Course Practice Test Items		Remediation	
			McDougal Littell Geometry	McDougal Littell Geometry Concepts & Skills
R.4.G.6 Solve problems using inscribed and circumscribed figures	ITEM	59, 60	5.2 10.3 10.4 11.5 12.3	11.5
	CORRECT	___/2		
R.4.G.7 Use orthographic drawings (top, front, side) and isometric drawings (corner) to represent three dimensional objects	ITEM	61, D	Project for Chapters 2 and 3 pp. 188–189	3.1 9.1 9.2 9.3 9.4 9.5
	CORRECT	___/2		
R.4.G.8 Draw, examine, and classify cross-sections of three dimensional objects	ITEM	62, 63	12.1 12.4 12.6	9.6
	CORRECT	___/2		
CGT.5.G.1 Use coordinate geometry to find the distance between two points, the midpoint of a segment, and the slopes of parallel, perpendicular, horizontal, and vertical lines	ITEM	65, 66, 67, 68, 69	1.3 1.5 3.6 3.7	2.1 3.6 4.4
	CORRECT	___/5		
CGT.5.G.2 Write equations of lines in slope-intercept form and use slope to determine parallel and perpendicular lines	ITEM	70, 71, 72, E	3.6 3.7	3.6
	CORRECT	___/4		
CGT.5.G.3 Determine, given a set of points, the type of figure based on its properties (parallelogram, isosceles triangle, trapezoid)	ITEM	73, 74, 75	6.4 6.5 6.6	6.3 6.6
	CORRECT	___/3		
CGT.5.G.4 Write, in standard form, the equation of a circle given a graph on a coordinate plane or the center and radius of a circle	ITEM	76, 77	10.6	11.7
	CORRECT	___/2		

Copyright © by McDougal Littell, a division of Houghton Mifflin Company.

Arkansas Learning Expectations	End-of-Course Practice Test Items	Remediation	
		McDougal Littell Geometry	McDougal Littell Geometry Concepts & Skills
CGT.5.G.5 Draw and interpret the results of transformations and successive transformations on figures in the coordinate plane: • translations • reflections • rotations (90°, 180°, clockwise and counterclockwise about the origin) • dilations (scale factor)	ITEM 78, 79, 80 CORRECT ___/3	7.1 7.2 7.3 7.4 7.5 8.7	3.7 5.7 7.6 11.8

Copyright © by McDougal Littell, a division of Houghton Mifflin Company.

Preparation for the Arkansas End of Course Exam for Geometry 89